FREE DAYS OUT
IN THE NORTH WEST

Free Days Out
in the North West

PETER HADDINGTON

Assistant Editor
Elisabeth Rowlatt

Editorial Assistant
Brenda Joynson

Wharncliffe Books

First Published in 2002 by
Wharncliffe Books
an imprint of
Pen and Sword Books Limited,
47 Church Street, Barnsley,
South Yorkshire. S70 2AS

*For up-to-date information on other titles produced under the
Wharncliffe imprint, please telephone or write to:*

> Wharncliffe Books
> FREEPOST
> 47 Church Street
> Barnsley
> South Yorkshire S70 2BR
> Telephone (24 hours): 01226 - 734555

ISBN: 1-903425-00-X

A CIP catalogue record of this book is available from the
British Library

Cover pictures: Front: *Castleton* (Kath Hodgson); *Birkenhead Park* (Heather Bradshaw); *Lady Lever Art Gallery* (Heather Bradshaw); *Worsley* (Ken Matthews); *Liverpool's waterfront* (David Williams). Back: *The Trafford Centre*.

Cover design: Paul Wilkinson

Printed in the United Kingdom by
CPI UK

Contents

The new footbridge across part of the Castleford Canal Basin in Manchester. Keith Warrender

Introduction

This book is primarily designed to help people plan interesting day trips that do not involve them in spending a lot of money. Herein is listed a wealth of free admission places in the North West, from Lancaster in the north to Nantwich in the south, from Liverpool and the Wirral in the west to the Pennines in the east.

The book is aimed, in particular, at two types of tourist. Those people who, although being able to afford to run a car, do not have a large amount left over to spend on leisure activities. And there are many folk who, despite having adequate funds, are careful with their money (to make sure they are comfortable in their old age, perhaps).

My wife and I recently paid a visit to a famous stately home, and were obliged to hand over a substantial entrance fee to view the house and gardens. We came away regretting that we had spent the money. There was a lake and lawns, but the gardens consisted of just one herbaceous border. Perhaps because the owners were still in residence, only a few rooms in the magnificent house were open to the public, and one could only view certain of the rooms from roped-off doorways.

On the other hand, a visit to a free admission attraction such as Chester Cathedral and the city walls forcibly reminds us that we do not need to spend a large sum of money in order to enjoy a truly memorable day out.

In this book are listed art galleries, museums, the odd free admission mansion, craft centres and large garden centres with special attractions. There are country parks, nature reserves and lovely villages which are large enough to occupy the visitor for some time. There are mill shops and special shopping and leisure centres like the Trafford Centre, near Manchester. I also list a number of outstanding municipal parks, plus cathedrals and important churches, which are open every day. Several historic towns, which are well worth exploring, are also mentioned.

One advantage of visiting places with free admission is that one can better afford to dine out on a trip, which is something which partners and parents really appreciate.

Also listed here, month-by-month, are major annual events in the region which are both free and well worth a visit.

I have also listed free admission venues in separate areas that are in and around the larger towns. Thus, if motorists are planning a visit to, for example, the Blackburn area they can see at a glance the variety of attractions in that area and be able to visit several places in one day.

At the time of writing all the places mentioned were quoting free admission, with the exception of passing references to other attractions nearby, which may involve an admission charge and in such cases, this is clearly stated. The reader will also find details of special low cost fees such as those in Liverpool, where a £3 annual ticket may be purchased which provides unlimited access to eight major art galleries and museums.

Apart from such situations as that in Liverpool, if you are required to pay an admission fee, this will have been imposed after compilation of this book, so I accept no responsibility!

While this book is up-to-date for 2002, readers are advised to telephone for information about attractions before setting out on lengthy journeys. This particularly applies to opening times, which may vary from year to year. Some small art galleries close temporarily between exhibitions.

At the present time the City of Manchester is preparing to stage the 2002 Commonwealth Games. During the Games, athletes from seventy-two nations will take part in seventeen sports. Many of these events will take place in the magnificent new City of Manchester Stadium, which has been built in east Manchester alongside Ashton New Road (A662).

The Games run from the Opening Ceremony on Saturday, 25 July 2002, to the Closing Ceremony on 4 August 2002. Events which can be watched free include the men's and women's Marathon on 28 July, starting and finishing at the Games Stadium. Also free is the Triathlon at Salford Quays on 4 August, (swimming, cycling and running). Other free events in the northwest include walking races in Manchester, and mountain biking and cycling road races at Rivington, near Horwich.

Schedules of events are obtainable from the Commonwealth Games Office at Heron House, Albert Square (opposite Manchester Town Hall). For further information about the Games, telephone the Games Information Line on 0870 609 2002, or the Commonwealth Games Office on 0161 220 2002.

Happy free days out!

Peter Haddington

Acknowledgements
The author thanks Bill Slater of Liverpool for supplying most of the pictures about Merseyside and all the pictures on Chester.

Accrington

OSWALDTWISTLE MILLS, Oswaldtwistle, Accrington

This single storey Victorian weaving mill has been turned into a large crafts centre which now occupies an area which in 1905 housed around 1,000 looms. The mill pools, or lodges, are also used as a wildfowl reserve, with a short circular walk.

During 2001 there was free admission to the Textile Time Tunnel museum, and hopefully this will continue. The museum tells the story of the rise and fall of the industry. There is a traditional sweet factory on this site. Textiles were woven here up to 2001, but the twenty-six looms were then moved to a mill at Blackburn. However, retail space at Oswaldtwistle Mills is being doubled.

James Hargreaves, inventor of the Spinning Jenny, was an ancestor of the Hargreaves family, who own and still operate Oswaldtwistle Mills, which was formerly known as Moscow Mill.

Location: Collier Street, just off Oswaldtwistle's main street, Union Street.

Opening times: Open seven days a week. Monday to Saturday 10.00 am to 5.00 pm, Sunday 11.00 am to 5.00 pm.

Telephone: 01254 871025.

Full disabled access available.

Laughing stock: While still in Oswaldtwistle, take a look at the amusing bronze sculptures on stone plinths in the village centre. Here are teapots, football boots, a loaf of bread, a hot water bottle, and other everyday objects. The £50,000 scheme to place these sculptures in the town was described as 'a monstrosity' during a local council meeting, while readers of the local paper, protested that the village centrepiece had made Oswaldtwistle 'a laughing stock'. The somewhat comic name of this town, apparently denotes a fork between two rivers.

HAWORTH ART GALLERY, Haworth Park, Manchester Road, Accrington

Accrington's art gallery began its existence as a lovely Edwardian stone mansion. It was built in the Tudor style and completed in 1909, as the home of textile manufacturer William Haworth and his sister Anne. In 1920, following the deaths of William and Hannah Haworth, the house was left to the people of Accrington. From the

The Haworth Art Gallery, Accrington. Garth Dawson

park there is a splendid view of the surrounding countryside. All in all, a delightful setting.

Inside the house is one of the finest collections of Tiffany art glass, tiles and ceramics in public hands outside North America. This collection is somewhat for the specialist and the display will be unlikely to impress the non-specialist viewer. The history of the collection is quite fascinating, as it was given to the town by Accrington born Joseph Briggs, who became manager of the Tiffany studio, in New York.

Location: On A680 to Haslingden, on the outskirts of Accrington.
Opening times: 2.00 pm to 5.00 pm six days a week. (closed Fridays).
Telephone: 01524 233782.
Partial disabled access only.

HOLDEN WOOD ANTIQUES, Haslingden

The former St Stephen's Church, Haslingden has been restored, and at the time of writing housed forty stalls selling antique furniture, ceramics, books, painting, clocks and jewellery. A veritable browsers' delight. There is also a tea room on the premises.

St Stephen's Church was originally built in 1867 at Crowtrees Village. After the village declined, the church was dismantled in 1925 and later re-erected half a mile away on its present site. The church closed and was de-consecrated in 1986. In 1995 it was purchased and subsequently converted for use as a retail antiques centre.

Location: Grane Road.

Opening times: Open seven days a week, 10.00 am to 5.30 pm.

Telephone: 01706 830803.

Partial disabled access only.

St Stephen's Church at Haslingden. It is now occupied by Holden Wood Antiques.

ACCRINGTON MARKETS

Accrington's Market Hall in Blackburn Road, Accrington (just behind the Town Hall), contains approximately seventy stalls offering a wide variety of goods. Opened in 1868, it has an impressive stone façade and is one of the finest buildings in the town.

Opening times: Open daily, except Wednesday. Sunday 9.00 am to 2.30 pm.
Open Market: Tuesday, Friday and Saturday 9.00 am to 4.00 pm.
Flea market: Thursday 9.00 am to 3.00 pm.
Telephone: 01254 233816.

WINFIELDS, Hazel Mill, Blackburn Road, Haslingden

This is a cut-price factory outlet, which claims to have the largest collection of footwear in the country, with over 100,000 pairs on show, plus clothing. There is a self-service restaurant on the site.

Opening times: Open seven days a week. Monday, Tuesday, Wednesday and Friday, 10.00 am to 5.30 pm. Thursday, 10.00 am to 8.00 pm. Saturday, 9.00 am to 5.30 pm. Sunday, 11.00 am to 5.00 pm.
Telephone: 01706 227916.

Full disabled access available.

Birkenhead

WIRRAL MUSEUM, Birkenhead

The impressive Birkenhead Town Hall has been transformed into a wonderful free admission museum which occupies the whole of the three storey building. Wirral Borough Council now uses Wallasey Town Hall as its administrative headquarters.

The museum at Birkenhead, which had been ten years in the making, opened its doors early in 2001. Apart from the exhibits, visitors can admire the brilliant architecture of the Town Hall, including the magnificent main staircase and the fabulous stained glass windows. The Grade I listed building is in the massive Hamilton Square. Buildings in the Square have been cleaned and restored to their former glory. They stand around beautiful central gardens. The Museum's exhibits cover both Birkenhead and the Wirral.

Opening times: Tuesday to Sunday 10.00 am to 5.00 pm.

Telephone: 0151 666 4010.

Full disabled access available.

WILLIAMSON ART GALLERY AND MUSEUM, Birkenhead

The Williamson Art Gallery and Museum was the pride of Birkenhead when it was first opened in 1928. The large single-storey, windowless, building was erected through the generosity of John Williamson, a director of the Cunard Steamship Company, and his son Patrick, who between them financed this marvellous purpose built arts complex.

Although the gallery is at Oxton, some way from the town centre, it is well worth finding! It contains fourteen exhibition galleries and a sculpture hall. Particular attention is devoted to the works of English watercolour artists, works by local artists of local scenes. There are also displays of English and Oriental ceramics, including Della Robbia pottery produced in Birkenhead and Liverpool porcelain. There is also an excellent gallery of large oils on canvas.

Museum exhibits include model boats, trams, veteran motorcycles and cars.

Location: Slatey Road, Oxton (near Birkenhead Park).

Opening times: Tuesday to Sunday 1.00 pm to 5.00 pm. Plus Bank Holidays.

Telephone: 0151 652 4177.

Full disabled access available.

Birkenhead Town Hall from Hamilton Square Gardens. Bill Slater

BIRKENHEAD PRIORY AND ST MARY'S TOWER

Birkenhead Priory, founded in 1150 and for centuries home to
Benedictine monks, is in a strange setting. It is bordered on its
riverside site by heavy industry. During our visit we were much aware
of huge yellow shipyard cranes, looming over the ancient buildings.

Much of the Priory is in ruins or has long since been demolished, and much of the stone removed. However, there is an interesting exhibition in the former crypt, which shows the history of the Priory, with interesting artefacts preserved and stained glass windows. The Chapter House, one of the few intact buildings on the site, is still used regularly for religious services. During our visit, an attendant kindly unlocked the entrance to the Chapter House, allowing us to gaze at the fine sandstone interior which has been in use for so many centuries.

In 1821 a new Church, St. Mary's, was built and consecrated on the Priory site. Sadly the only part of this which remains intact, is the tower. The attendant unlocked the door of this and my wife and I did what all visitors should do. We climbed the 101 steps to the viewing balcony at the top of the tower, which is then topped by a steeple. We enjoyed a fabulous view of the Mersey across to Liverpool Pier Head and along the river. Looking straight down, we saw next to the Priory, a large ship in Laird's dry dock, with 'ants' swarming over the deck.

Birkenhead Priory was initially established for sixteen monks and in its early days, they offered free food and shelter to travellers, before rowing or sailing them across the Mersey. The Priory buildings, with their cloisters, were not completed until the fourteenth century.

The Priory was forcibly closed in 1536 as part of the dissolution of the monasteries during the reign of King Henry VIII. Like many other priors in those times, John Sharpe, Prior for seventeen years, was given a pension, but the ordinary monks had to leave and find jobs where they could. It is said that in their anxiety to save the Priory's treasures, some monks used an underground passage in an attempt to escape with the valuables. The story has it that as they attempted to escape through the tunnel, a great stone fell and blocked the passage crushing one monk and entombing others.

Location: Between Birkenhead Tunnel entrance and river.

Opening times: Saturday and Sunday 1.00 pm to 5.00 pm all year. All school holidays: Open Tuesday to Friday as well as weekends.

Telephone: 0151 666 1249.

Partial disabled access only.

BIRKENHEAD PARK

Opened in 1847 and designed by Joseph Paxton, head gardener at Chatsworth, this glorious place was Britain's first publicly owned park. It was the inspiration for Central Park in New York.

Now it is to be restored to its Victorian glory with the help of a thumping £6M Lottery Grant. Paxton created a Little Eden here

The lower lake boathouse at Birkenhead Park. Mike Garrett

The lower lake boathouse at Birkenhead Park. Heather Bradshaw

with two lakes, rockeries, summer houses, grottos and romantic bridges. The park features two cricket grounds and the headquarters of Birkenhead Park RUFC (founded 1846).

Location: Between Park Road South and Park Road North, not far from the town centre.

Annual hot air balloon festival in Birkenhead Park. Heather Bradshaw

BIDSTON HILL

Situated at the back of Birkenhead near the M53, Bidston Hill is a 231 ft high ridge. On top of the hill is a former lighthouse (1872), and a windmill which ceased working in 1875. The windmill is open to the public on the first Sunday of each month (2.00 pm to 4.00 pm).

The lighthouse ceased operations in 1913, after being a guide to mariners for 142 years. There is also a former observatory on Bidston Hill. Built in 1866 and initially fitted with telescopes which are now in Liverpool Museum, this building is now a marine research laboratory.

Farm: On the side of Bidston Hill, is the Tam O'Shanter Urban Farm, which is open to the public daily. There is a variety of animals for the visitor to see.

Good views of Merseyside can be had from the footpath along the top of Bidston Hill.

Bidston Hill Windmill, Birkenhead.
Bill Slater

Farm opening times: 9.30 am to 4.30 pm.
Location: Boundary Road, off Upton Road (A5027).
Telephone: 0151 653 9332.

BIRKENHEAD MARKET

This large Market Hall was built in 1977, following a huge fire that left the old market a smouldering heap in 1974.
Location: Conway Road.
Opening times: Monday to Saturday 9.00 am to 5.00 pm.

EGERTON BRIDGE, Birkenhead

A tram ride away from the Woodside Visitor Centre on the waterfront is the restored Egerton Bridge. Climb the iron stairway for a birds-eye view over dockland. This is one of the famous Mersey Bascule bridges. Restored machine house and video history of Birkenhead.
Location: End of Shore Road.
Opening times: Saturday and Sunday only, 1.00 pm to 5.00 pm. (winter 12.00 pm to 4.00 pm).

Blackburn

BLACKBURN CATHEDRAL

Blackburn is home to one of England's newest Cathedrals. Originally the Parish Church of Blackburn (erected in 1826) it became a Cathedral in 1926, when the Diocese of Blackburn was founded from the northern part of the Diocese of Manchester.

In 1938 work began on extending the old parish church to fit its role as a Cathedral. Transepts were added and the church also extended eastward. Outstanding features of the Cathedral include the fourteenth century misericordes, reputedly from Whalley Abbey; the massive oak Ramsay pulpit, given by a local doctor of that name and the Bishop's Throne in oak (produced by craftsmen at Tideswell village, Derbyshire).

Location: Blackburn Cathedral is in the centre of town, adjacent to the railway station.

Opening times: Open to visitors every day from 8.30 am to 5.00 pm.

Telephone: 01254 51491.

BLACKBURN MUSEUM AND ART GALLERY,
Museum Street

The drive to Blackburn from Manchester can follow either motorway routes north, or the 'cross country' route north on the A666. It is always enjoyable to potter round an unfamiliar town centre. One of the many surprises that Blackburn town centre offers is the realisation that the beautiful stone façade of the former Blackburn Cotton Exchange, now provides a beautiful façade for a cinema. Movies with elegance!

Blackburn Museum and Art Gallery occupies a stone faced building that was originally erected as a Carnegie library. The museum, which is on the ground floor, houses displays of local and natural history, a display covering the history of the East Lancashire Regiment and an Asian section which reflects the modern town's significant Asian population. There is a special display relating to Victoria Cross hero Marcus Ervine-Andrew, who won the only VC awarded as a result of the Dunkirk evacuation in 1940.

The fine collection of nineteenth century British paintings in the Art Gallery on the first floor, failed to inspire this visitor, but that is more a reflection on my taste than the works on view. The adjacent gallery contains the magnificent Hart coin collection, plus several

illuminated manuscripts and ancient books. Edward Hart, a wealthy Blackburn rope manufacturer, gifted thousands of Greek, Roman and early British coins to the town.
Opening times: Tuesday to Friday, noon to 4.45 pm Saturday 9.45 am to 4.45 pm.
Telephone: 01254 667130.
Full disabled access available.

LEWIS TEXTILE MUSEUM, Exchange Street
The collection of preserved textile machinery is housed behind glass on the ground floor. Machinery on display ranges from original hand looms to relatively modern power looms. At the time of writing there were no picture displays or relics of the proud cotton weaving centre which Blackburn once was. There were expansion plans at the time of our visit, so a check to determine exactly what is available for the visitor to view may be prudent.

The upstairs gallery of the building houses regularly changing displays and we were lucky enough to view a marvellous collection of framed photographs, taken by local press photographers during the previous fifty years. This public building was formerly a cafe and billiard hall and is situated just round the corner from Blackburn Museum.
Opening times: Tuesday to Friday noon to 4.45 pm. Saturday 9.45 am to 4.45 pm.
Telephone: 01254 667130.
Partial disabled access only.

BLACKBURN MARKETS COMPLEX
Markets daily except Sundays.
Main market on Wednesday, Friday and Saturday.
Rooftop car park.
Location: In town centre. Building bounded by Ainsworth Street, Brown Street and Penny Street.
Telephone: 01254 52911.

SUNNYHURST WOOD AND VISITOR CENTRE
Sunnyhurst Wood lies in a steep-sided valley between the high moors of Winter Hill and Darwen Hill, the latter surmounted by the famous Darwen Tower. The wood covers eighty-five acres and provides the walker with seven miles of footpaths, although some of these are quite close to each other. The paths are all sheltered from the bitter winds, which can often be encountered during winter. The wood,

through which a brook flows, was acquired for the town by public subscription, to commemorate the coronation of Edward VII in 1902.

The old keeper's cottage now serves as the Visitor Centre, while the upstairs gallery of this building is a popular exhibition venue for local artists. Near the Visitor Centre is the Tudor-style 'Old England' cafe, which serves full meals.

Our visit was in February and it was necessary to shelter from torrential rain under a bandstand-like cover in Sunnyhurst Wood, along with twenty-five other ramblers. The walk leader had taken us over the moors in freezing February weather and we descended only briefly into the wood to eat our sandwiches, our walk leader, had ignored a warm and welcoming pub, which beckoned as we squelched past. Clearly, a not universal hardiness is required of those embarking on these guided moorland walks!

Location: Just west of Darwen, off A666.

Opening times: The visitor centre is usually open on Tuesdays, Thursdays, Saturdays and Sundays between 2.00 pm and 4.30 pm.

Telephone: 01254 701545.

WITTON COUNTRY PARK

Witton Country Park covers 480 acres of land, of which approximately half is mixed wood and parkland, while the rest is farmland or rough grassland with open public access. The Visitor Centre includes restored stables, harness room and coach house. On show are permanent displays of nineteenth century horse-drawn carriages, old farm machinery and a natural history room. There are also regularly changed exhibitions and a tea room.

The estate was once owned by the Feilden family, who built Witton House, which was demolished in 1954, as a result of it falling into decay. The estate was purchased by Blackburn Corporation in 1946.

Location: Witton Country Park is on the west side of town (main entrance on A674 road to Chorley).

Opening times: Visitor Centre open every day from April to September. Open Thursday to Sunday during October to March.

Telephone: 01254 55423.

Blackpool

GRUNDY ART GALLERY, Queen Street, Blackpool

Purpose-built in 1911, the Grundy Art Gallery is described as 'one of the most delightful small galleries in the country'. The exhibits regularly on view include a large collection given to the town in 1903 by the brothers John and Cuthbert Grundy.

Visitors are able to view Victorian oils and watercolours, contemporary prints, modern British paintings, oriental ivories, ceramics and photographs of old Blackpool, plus regularly changed special exhibitions.

Location: Queen Street is off the promenade opposite the North Pier. There is a 'Pay and Display' car park next to the Art Gallery.

Opening times: Monday to Saturday 10.00 am to 5.00 pm all year. Closed Sundays and Bank Holidays.

Telephone: 01253 751701.

Full disabled access available.

STANLEY PARK, West Park Drive, Blackpool

Blackpool is an urban resort, which is not noted for its greenery, but it possesses one magnificent oasis of greenery in Stanley Park, a place well worth visiting. This is a massive park with a large and beautiful boating lake, Italian gardens, rose gardens, conservatories and a host of sports facilities. There is also a good cafe and a Model Village, (there is an admission charge to the village).

The park, which covers 256 acres and includes its own golf course, occupies land bought by Blackpool Corporation during the 1920s. It is named after the Lord Derby who opened it in 1926 (his full name was Edward George Villiers Stanley). On completion, Stanley Park was one of the most comprehensive municipal park schemes ever carried out in Britain.

Location: Stanley Park is at the back of the town centre on the A587 bounded by West Park Drive, East Park Drive and North Park Drive.

BLACKPOOL PLEASURE BEACH

Claimed to be Britain's No. 1 free admission attraction in terms of number of visitors. This huge fairground site also has a large number of shops, bars and restaurants.

Location: Beside Promenade at South end of Blackpool's built-up area.

Blackpool Pleasure Beach at night.

Richard Rodriguez, who lives in the United States, celebrates reaching the halfway mark on his World Record Rollercoaster Marathon at Blackpool Pleasure Beach. He completed a record 2000 hours for the year 2000.

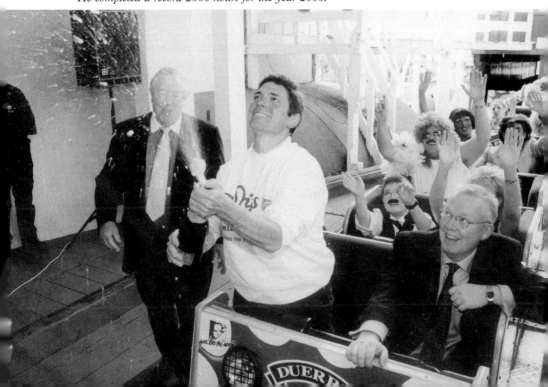

The stone front of Valhalla, the big new attraction for 2000 at Blackpool Pleasure Beach.

BLACKPOOL ILLUMINATIONS

Originally displayed on Princess Parade in May 1912, to celebrate the first Royal visit to Blackpool by Princess Louise. The Princess officially opened a new section of the promenade subsequently known as Princess Parade. Approximately 10,000 lamps were used in this colourful display. The 'lights' were such a success that the local Chamber of Commerce and other business people persuaded the Council to stage them again in September of that year.

The 'lights' were then staged again in 1913 but the First World War prevented continuation of this idea. However, the Illuminations were resumed again in 1925.

Today, there are 5³/₄ miles of lights between Squires Gate and Bispham. The main tableaux are on display at Bispham, Blackpool's north end. The best way of seeing the spectacle is to take a tram from Blackpool Tower to Bispham and then walk back to the Tower. The Illuminations are on display from the beginning of September through to the first week of November.

Blackpool Illuminations, which started in the nineteenth century. Kath Hodgson

BLACKPOOL'S PIERS
Blackpool's North, Central and South Piers are all free admission. They boast a heady mixture of amusement arcades, fun fairs, shops, restaurants and bars. All the piers have theatres.
Opening times: Easter to the first week in November.
Note: There is a smaller Pier at nearby St Anne's on Sea.

MARTON MERE NATURE RESERVE, Blackpool
Marton Mere is the most important habitat on the Fylde peninsula for breeding and wintering birds. It is also on a major migration route and rare species appear frequently. Thirty acres of open water, are surrounded by reed beds, with some seventy acres of marsh grassland and developing woodland also within the reserve. There is a small Visitor Centre.
Location: Between Blackpool Zoo and the National Stocks and Bonds computer building. Approached along East Park Drive, turning into Lawson Road.

WREA GREEN, near Blackpool

Wrea Green lies midway between Blackpool and Preston. It is an idyllic and unspoiled English village, complete with pond and green. Around the green stands the church, pub, school, village pump and a farm. There is also a windmill, now converted into a house.

Location: Wrea Green is a mile or so south of the A583 Blackpool to Preston road, on B5259. Roughly one mile west of the market town of Kirkham.

FREEPORT SHOPPING AND LEISURE VILLAGE
Anchorage Road, Fleetwood

Cut-price factory outlet goods is the name of the game at Freeport Shopping and Leisure Village. This purpose built centre has given Fleetwood a long awaited commercial boost. Visitors can buy famous name goods here at up to fifty per cent off recommended retail prices.

Opened in 1995, Freeport is off the A585, just outside the town and beside the river Wyre. It lies next to the river marina, so boats are also part of the scene here. There is a tropical butterfly house (admission charges apply), go-karts, a playground for children, with rides and restaurants.

Opening times: Freeport is open seven days a week from 9.30 am.

FLEETWOOD MARKET

Consists of over 250 stalls.

Opening times: From July to October, the market is open six days a week, (closed Wednesdays).

Telephone: 01253 771651.

Bolton

BOLTON CENTRAL MUSEUM, ART GALLERY AND AQUARIUM

The glorious stone faced Crescent behind Bolton Town Hall is partly occupied by a four-in-one complex comprising a museum, art gallery, library and aquarium.

The museum is notable for its collection of ancient Egyptian artefacts, including mummies from both Egypt and Peru. The museum also features a marvellous natural history collection of stuffed birds and animals. The basement aquarium is also well worth visiting.

Bolton Town Hall. Bolton Evening News

The wonderful Crescent was built in the 1930s. It lies behind the equally impressive Town Hall, completed in 1873. Another outstanding feature of Bolton is the *Bolton Evening News*. Launched in 1867 it was the first evening newspaper in Britain not connected to a morning newspaper (apart from the *Daily Shipping Gazette* at South Shields).

Opening times: Monday to Friday 9.30 am to 5.30 pm, (closed Wednesdays), Saturday 10.00 am to 5.00 pm.

Telephone: 01204 332194.

Full disabled access available.

ANIMAL WORLD AND BUTTERFLY WORLD, Moss Bank Park, Bolton

In 1994 the Park's pets' corner was modernised and a tropical butterfly house was added to the existing attractions. The result is an excellent miniature zoo, which is an extremely popular attraction, especially on a fine Sunday.

The small animals and birds are splendidly housed, with particular protection from vandals and stray domestic pets, by an eleven foot high fence topped with razor wire. Clearly, an expensive, but a sadly necessary defence. The exotic butterflies in the free flight house are imported in pupa form from breeding centres in, among other places, Costa Rica, the Philippines and Thailand, becoming butterflies in Bolton.

Near Animal World is Moss Bank Park's other outstanding feature, the hillside rock garden, with rocky paths and water cascading down to an ornamental pond.

Location: Moss Bank Park is a mile from Bolton town centre, in the north-western outskirts of the town. The main entrance is on Moss Bank Way (A58), a busy ring road. Animal World is open seven days a week, usually from 10.00 am to 4.30 pm.

Telephone: 01204 334121.

Full disabled access available.

SMITHILLS HALL AND SMITHILLS COACHING HOUSE

Near Moss Bank Park is fourteenth century Smithills Hall (there is an admission charge here), and Smithills Coaching House (a renowned restaurant). It is worth walking round the outside of Smithills Hall and its garden, and there is a nature trail running through nearby woodland.

BOLTON MARKETS

Of all the big towns in the Manchester area, none can better the

The Last Drop Village, on the moors near Bolton. Kath Hodgson

excellence of Bolton as a shopping centre. Bolton's many large department stores and fabulous indoor market are all within a compact area making for easy shopping. The Indoor Market in Corporation Street has in recent years been rebuilt to a high standard, with new stalls set well apart, providing acres of walking space for shoppers.

Opening times: Open seven days a week. Monday to Saturday 9.00 am to 5.00 pm, Sunday 10.00 am to 4.00 pm.

On the other side of Bolton Town Hall, are **Ashburner Street indoor and outdoor markets,** selling fish, vegetables and clothes.
Opening times: Open Tuesday, Thursday and Saturday. 8.30 am to 4.30 pm. There is a partial opening on Fridays.

JUMBLES COUNTRY PARK, near Bolton

This country park comprises Jumbles Reservoir and the surrounding hilly countryside. There is a walk of nearly two miles round the reservoir. The route of the countryside walk is on higher ground, away from the reservoir, on part of its western shore.

You can also walk north from the reservoir alongside Bradshaw Brook, to the village of Turton Bottoms. From here it is a short walk to the big Wayoh Reservoir and a further walk brings visitors to the Turton and Entwistle Reservoir, set in grand moorland scenery.

Location: The main entrance to Jumbles Country Park is on Bradshaw Road (the A676 to Ramsbottom). Jumbles is three miles north of central Bolton.

The park is open from dawn to dusk all year round. There is a Visitor Centre.

LEVER PARK, Horwich, near Bolton

The visitor to Lever Park is able to enjoy a scenic drive along country lanes around four large reservoirs, followed by tea at the picturesque Great House Barn in Lever Park. Thousands of visitors come at weekends, weather permitting, so go midweek if you are seeking solitude!

The Great House Barn, which is understood to date from the Middle Ages, is supported by huge cruck beams and is definitely a cafe with a difference. Nearby is a gift shop and art gallery and from here paths lead in all directions through woodland.

Not far away is Rivington Hall, available for pre booked functions only and not generally open to the public. Rivington Hall Barn is now a restaurant. On the banks of Lower Rivington Reservoir stands a replica of Liverpool Castle, which once stood in the centre of that city. At the north end of Lever Park is Rivington village with its sixteenth century parish church.

The village is a charming spot at the junction of the Lower and Upper Rivington Reservoirs, and in addition the Anglezarke and Yarrow reservoirs complete a scene worthy of the Lake District. High on Rivington Moor stands the famous Rivington Pike tower, built in 1773 by the owner of Rivington Hall. The Pike is a traditional climb for picnickers, especially at Easter, and can be reached from the Great House Barn.

From the rear of Rivington Hall a footpath leads up the side of Rivington Moor to the terraced hillside gardens, which were constructed by William Hesketh Lever, otherwise known as Lord Leverhulme, the Bolton man who made his fortune from Sunlight Soap. He planted thousands of bushes and trees to act as wind breaks on what was otherwise an inhospitable heather-covered slope, thus sheltering his garden from the harsh climate. The grounds include a lake, a Japanese garden and a ravine crossed by a stone bridge.

In 1900, Lord Leverhulme bought the manor of Rivington for the then enormous sum of £60,000, and shortly afterwards built a large timber bungalow and started work on the gardens. In 1913 a suffragette set fire to the bungalow, destroying it. Later, Lord

Leverhulme built a palatial stone bungalow on the site of the original timber structure. This was eventually demolished in 1948 by the later landowners, Liverpool Corporation Waterworks. The gardens, long neglected and overgrown, have been partially restored.

Location: Lever Park is about a mile away from the M61 (junction 6 near Horwich). The A673 Bolton to Chorley road passes near the entrance to Lever Park.

Opening times: Dawn to dusk.

MOSES GATE COUNTRY PARK, Farnworth, near Bolton

This attractive area, lying beside the river Croal, was created on the site of a hideous industrial tip, almost moon-like in its desolation. Even Rock Hall, now the Visitor centre, had become semi-derelict before its restoration. This fine Georgian house was built in 1806 for John Crompton, owner of a paper-making mill which once stood nearby.

Near Rock Hall are Crompton Lodges, three reservoirs created to serve the needs of the nearby paper mill. Today, various activities take place on and around these reservoirs including fishing, canoeing, dinghy sailing and sail boarding.

The country park extends to where the river Croal joins the river Irwell at Nob End, south of Rock Hall. It is now possible to walk down the Croal-Irwell valley, all the way from Bolton to Salford.

Location: The entrance to Moses Gate Country Park is on the A6053 between Moses Gate (Farnworth) and Little Lever.

Opening times: Dawn to dusk.

Visitor Centre: 01204 571561.

BARROW BRIDGE, Bolton

A picturesque hamlet nestling below the moorland just north of Bolton, Barrow Bridge was once a textile manufacturing centre, and latterly has become a favourite with day visitors.

It was constructed as a 'model village', built to give nineteenth century workers living conditions which were regarded as almost Utopian at the time the village was built. After the Second World War, people went in droves to the boating lake and cafe, regarding it as a grand day out. Sadly, the site of the lake, originally constructed as a reservoir for the mill, is now a car park.

The Dean Brook burbles past old stone cottages, first built for mill managerial staff, and there is a flight of sixty-three stone steps to climb at the end of the village. They were built to provide easy access for quarry and coal mine workers employed on the moors. Visitors can enjoy a circular walk starting from here, over the many moorland footpaths.

At the Bolton end of the village the visitor will find a steep flight of steps. At the top of these is a big surprise, the terraced homes built for the ordinary mill workers, and the school which was rather quaintly referred to as 'The Institute'. This was built in 1846. By 1850 the workers had also established a successful Co-op shop in the village.

A water powered carding mill built here during the eighteenth century, was demolished in the 1830s by industrialist Robert Gardner, who replaced it with two larger mills. The mill manager, under Gardner's direction, had erected, the excellent workers' houses, many of which stand today. The mills were eventually demolished in 1913.

Just below the moors, children of all ages delight in paddling in the wide brook at Barrow Bridge. It is an excellent spot for picnics, but there is no cafe or pub here.

Location: Barrow Bridge is off the A58 ring road in north Bolton, the other side of Moss Bank Park.

BARTON GRANGE GARDEN CENTRE, Deane, Bolton

This garden centre, situated on the outskirts of Bolton, is a member of the three-strong group which, in 1997, won the Garden Centre of the Year Award. Gifts galore are available in the extensive covered showrooms. There is also a small pets and aquarium section and an excellent restaurant.

Location: Wigan Road, Deane.

Opening times: Monday to Saturday 9.00 am to 5.30 pm. Sunday 10.30 am to 4.30 pm. Thursday 9.00am to 8.00 pm. (summer only).

Telephone: 01204 660660.

Full disabled access available.

HORWICH HERITAGE CENTRE

Changing displays about the history and industries of Horwich. The town below Rivington Pike was once an important railway repair centre. Occupying a former military barracks, the Heritage Centre is manned by volunteers.

Location: Longworth Road, off Chorley Old Road.

Opening times: Wednesdays 2.00 pm to 4.00 pm. Saturdays 10.00 am to 12.00 pm. Also second Tuesday of each month, 7.30 pm to 9.00 pm.

Telephone: 01204 847797.

Bury

BURY ART GALLERY AND MUSEUM

On view at Bury Art Gallery is one of the few complete collections of Victorian art on permanent display in the north west of England.

In 1897, seventeen years after the death of local paper manufacturer Thomas Wrigley, his children offered the pictures to the people of Bury, on condition that the town built what was to become the excellent Art Gallery in Moss Street, Bury. In the four spacious galleries there are many lovely and some very large oil paintings on view. The lower floor houses the museum, which is presented as Paradise Street with old shop and house interiors. Children will enjoy seeing the working model railway scene depicting Bury's two old railway stations, one which was in Bolton Street and the other in Knowsley Street.

It is intended to eventually move this museum to a more suitable town centre site, so that more exhibits can be brought out of store.

Location: In town centre near Kay Gardens.

Opening times: Tuesday to Saturday, 10.00 am to 5.00 pm all year. Closed Sunday and Monday.

Telephone: 0161 253 5878.

Full disabled access from the library around the corner (Textile Hall).

SUMMERSEAT GARDEN CENTRE

With four showrooms and plenty of outdoor space, this garden centre is in an attractive setting at the bottom of the Irwell Valley, two miles north of Bury town centre and near Summerseat railway

A steam train approaching Summerseat station, near Bury, on the East Lancashire Railway. Hugh Thom

Flashback to 1987, when this locomotive was used at the re-opening to steam passenger services of the East Lancashire Railway. Bury Council

station on the East Lancashire Steam Railway.
Location: Railway Street.
Opening times: Seven days a week, 9.00 am to 6.00 pm all year round. The cafe is open from 10.00 am to 4.00 pm.
Telephone: 01204 883048.

BURRS COUNTRY PARK, Bury
River Irwell and countryside walks just north of Bury town centre.

NEWBANK GARDEN CENTRE, Bury Road, Radcliffe
Businessman John Hartle bought Irwell Bank Farm in 1987 and it subsequently opened as a Garden Centre in 1992. When we visited, it had developed to cover some eight acres alongside the river. The farmhouse is now a fine restaurant. There are extensive showrooms packed with a vast array of plants and goods for the house and garden, from books to ceramics. The site features a separately owned aquatic centre.

Location: Off the A56 Manchester to Bury Road on to the A6053. Head towards Radcliffe for roughly half a mile. The Garden Centre can be found on the right.
Opening times: Monday to Thursday 9.30 am to 8.00 pm. Friday, Saturday and Sunday, 9.30 am to 5.30 pm.
Telephone: 0161 724 0585.

RAMSBOTTOM

The town of Ramsbottom is set amongst grand hilly scenery in the Irwell Valley, some four miles north of Bury. In recent years the town has enjoyed a major tourist 'facelift', coinciding with the return of the Age of Steam attraction.

The East Lancashire Railway now sends its puffing delights to Ramsbottom Station. Tourists often stand on the footbridge, which straddles the line to watch trains arrive and depart, while enveloping them in clouds of steam as they pass beneath. The locomotives run

A steam train of the East Lancashire Railway in Ramsbottom station. Kath Hodgson

An East Lancashire Railway steam train calls at Ramsbottom station. Hugh Thom

for eight miles between Bury and Rawtenstall.

Ramsbottom also has interesting shops and good cafes for those who tire of watching steam trains pass by. There is a small free admission museum at the Heritage Centre in Carr Street.

Opening times: Heritage Centre - Saturday and Sunday, 1.30 pm to 4.00 pm.

Telephone: 01706 821603.

Full disabled access available.

Burnley

TOWNELEY HALL ART GALLERY AND MUSEUMS, Burnley

Impressive Towneley Hall must be one of the most outstanding free admission mansions in Britain, and as such deserves a star billing in this book. We visited it on a lovely sunny Sunday in September, and it seemed as though half the population of Burnley had descended on the park, hall, local crafts museum and natural history centre. It was good to see so many people enjoying themselves without having to pay to get in. My wife correctly described the place as 'fabulous'.

When we entered the superb red Regency room of the hall, we found two ladies were playing lovely music on a grand piano and violin, reminding us of the splendid lifestyle of the Towneley family, owners of the property since the thirteenth century. The last male heir in the family died in 1877, and the Towneley estate was then split between six heiresses. The Hall became the property of Lady O'Hagan, who sold it to Burnley Corporation in 1902 to be used as a museum and art gallery.

Towneley Hall, Burnley. Garth Dawson

A small quantity of pictures and some furniture from the Towneley era remain in the house, but Burnley Council has filled the place with the town's art treasures. Visitors can see the massive, ornate entrance hall, two grand Regency rooms, the Long Gallery and adjacent bedrooms, kitchen, housekeeper's room and servants' dining room, family dining room, chapel, East Lancashire Regiment room and the art galleries. There are also pictures in most of the rooms.

The main art gallery contains large 'traditional', pictures, while in other galleries can be found visiting exhibitions. During our visit, the subjects included photography and wood sculpture. Also on show is a collection of rare cloth of gold vestments from Whalley Abbey, brought to Towneley Hall for safekeeping during the Reformation in the sixteenth century.

The Towneleys were Catholics and refused to give up their faith when Protestantism became the official religion during the reign of Elizabeth I. As a result, John Towneley (1528-1607) was fined and jailed for almost twenty-five years.

Museum of Crafts and Local Industries: This building, situated adjacent to the Hall, houses many interesting items, including Victorian bicycles, antique washing machines and an 1852 printing press, which was used to print the first edition of the *Burnley Advertiser*. The museum is only open on Sundays (when staff are available).

Natural History Centre and Aquarium: This building, situated in the old kitchen garden, is usually open seven days a week, although times may vary.

Towneley Hall park covers 500 acres and boasts both eighteen and nine hole golf courses, and an eighteen hole pitch and putt course. All three are open to the public. The park also offers fine scenic views of the surrounding countryside. There is a cafe near the Hall.

Towneley Hall is open all the year round.

Location: Park entrance one mile from Burnley town centre on A671, Bacup Road.

Opening times: Monday to Friday 10.00 am to 5.00 pm. Sundays 12 noon to 5.00 pm. Closed Saturdays.

Telephone: 01282 424213

Partial disabled access only.

HALL EXTENSION: At the time of writing, Burnley Council planned to build a low extension to the Hall in matching stone, to provide extra public facilities.

THE WEAVERS' TRIANGLE, Burnley

The 'triangle' in question is a well-preserved industrial townscape, centred on the Leeds and Liverpool Canal near Burnley town centre. The old buildings date from the days when Burnley led the world in the weaving of cotton cloth.

The canal wharf, like Wigan Pier, survives and the splendid Visitor Centre is located in the former Wharfmaster's House and Canal Toll office. There are pictures and exhibits from the days of King Cotton, a weaver's grim cellar dwelling, a Victorian parlour, and a hand-made wooden model fairground with moving parts. A former canal warehouse here is now *The Inn at Burnley Wharf*, and serves excellent meals.

Location: Manchester Road, 200 yards from Burnley Town Hall.
Opening times: The Visitor Centre opens from Easter to the end of September, Saturday to Wednesday inclusive. 2.00 pm to 4.00 pm. October - Sundays only 2.00 pm to 4.00 pm.
Telephone: 01282 452403.

Note: At the time of writing restoration work was being carried out on the Oak Mount Mill steam engine, prior to public display.

ROURKE'S FORGE, Burnley

Demonstrations by blacksmiths using forge, anvil and hammer are the highlight of a visit to the Vulcan Works. Iron furniture, gates, railings and decorative objects are made here. The firm was started in 1961 in a hen hut by Brian and Betty Rourke. Since 1994 the firm has achieved five gold awards and one silver award for outstanding design in craftsmanship. The site offers a visitor centre, extensive showrooms and a gift shop.

Location: Accrington Road, Burnley. (A679).
Opening times: Monday to Thursday 8.00 am to 5.00 pm. Friday and Saturday, 8.00 am to 4.00 pm.
Telephone: 01282 422841.
Partial disabled access only.

BURNLEY MARKETS

Burnley was granted a markets' charter as long ago as 1294.
Open market: Monday, Thursday, Saturday (Antiques on Wednesday). 9.00 am to 5.00 pm.
Market Hall: Open Monday to Saturday 9.00 am to 5.00 pm, but closed Tuesday.
The Market Hall in Curzon Street has more than 260 stalls.

SHERRY'S TOWEL MILL AND FACTORY SHOP, Padiham

One can see looms weaving top quality towelling products if one takes advantage of free guided tours at Stockbridge Mill at Padiham, near Burnley.

J & M Sherry opened up their mill to retail customers in 1992. If you wish to watch the manufacturing processes it is advisable to telephone the mill beforehand, to ensure that staff are available to take you and other visitors round. The mill shop sells a comprehensive range of household textiles and the cafe serves light refreshments.

Location: Stockbridge Road, Padiham.

Opening times: Monday to Friday 10.00 am to 5.30 pm. Saturday, 10.00 am to 5.00 pm. Sunday 10.00 am to 4.00 pm.

Factory tours - Monday to Friday only.

Telephone: 01282 774525.

Full disabled access available.

BARLEY, near Nelson

A few miles from Burnley stands the delightful village of Barley, which nestles at the foot of the 1827 ft Pendle Hill. It is from Barley that the most convenient ascent of Pendle to The Beacon is made, (climbing Pendle has always been a favourite Bank Holiday outing). This is the famous 'Lancashire Witches' country. (five women were hanged in 1612 after being convicted on witchcraft charges). There is a visitor centre in Barley, which tells the tale.

Around Barley are four reservoirs, which provide visitors with an easier walk than going up Pendle Hill. The village was once a textile mills centre.

Location: The village lies to the north of the A6068, Nelson to Padiham Road.

HOLLIN HALL SEWING CENTRE, Hollin Hall Mill, Trawden

Set in picturesque surroundings at the village of Trawden near Colne. There is an extensive mill shop, with free exhibitions. Excellent tea room.

Opening times: Monday to Friday 9.00 am to 5.00 pm, Saturday and Sunday 10.00 am to 4.00pm.

Telephone: 01282 863181.

Full disabled access available.

WYCOLLER COUNTRY PARK, near Colne

Wycoller Country Park is situated a few miles to the east of Colne, on the edge of the Pennines. The area has great scenic, historic, and, through its association with the Bronte sisters, considerable literary interest. The surrounding countryside and wild moors emphasize the character and appeal of Wycoller.

Places of interest to visit include the hamlet of Wycoller, the ruins of Wycoller Hall, the Country Park Visitor centre, Fosters Leap and Boulsworth Hill.

Location: From Colne take the A6068 eastward to Laneshawbridge, then turn right onto a minor road leading to Wycoller.

Opening times: Dawn to dusk.

PENDLE ARTS GALLERY, Barrowford

Pendle Heritage Centre occupies a former detached stone house beside Pendle Water at Barrowford, near Colne. The Pendle Arts Gallery is part of the Heritage Centre and admission to the Gallery is free. The Gallery stages temporary exhibitions of paintings and photographs, many by local artists and photographers.

It is open daily but it may close while exhibitions are being changed.

The Heritage Centre also includes a museum, walled garden and ancient cruck barn, but there are admission charges to these.

There is also a tea room and gift shop.

Location: Park Hill, Barrowford, next to Barrowford Park (M65, junction 13 onto the A682 to the junction with B6247).

Opening times: Arts Gallery is open seven days a week, 10.00 am to 5.00 pm.

Telephone: 01282 661701.

No specific disabled access.

Chester

CHESTER CATHEDRAL

Chester Cathedral must surely be one of the best loved in Britain. Visit this glorious monument in sandstone in the summer and you will see tourists from all parts of Britain and indeed from all over the world.

Following a delightful afternoon viewing the many ecclesiastical treasures, we invested £2.50 in a copy of the excellent guidebook on sale in the cathedral. (How could one leave without giving the cathedral something?).

Even the restaurant here is housed in a magnificent hall, which was once the refectory for forty monks.

Chester Cathedral stands on the site of a tenth century Saxon church, dedicated to St Werburgh, daughter of the Mercian King Wulfere. She became a nun and later rose to become an abbess. In 1092 the church became a Benedictine Abbey, and a new building in the Norman style was erected, parts of which still stand. This church was gradually rebuilt from about 1250 onwards. The process took 250 years and resulted in the building we see today.

Following the dissolution of the monasteries by Henry VIII, the Abbey was closed in 1540, but in the following year, it became the cathedral of the newly formed Diocese of Chester.

The delicate woodwork of the choir stalls dates from 1380 and is among the finest surviving medieval woodwork in Britain. Each of the canopies is different from its neighbour. There are also beautifully carved misericordes (small ledges) on the backs of the seats, helping the monks to stand during the extremely long services so common in those times. The fabulous golden ceiling dates from 1880, and was cleaned in 1989.

In the nave there are marvellous wall mosaic panels depicting Old Testament characters. These panels date from 1883. The Westminster stained glass windows on the south side of the nave were installed in 1992, having been given to the cathedral by the Duke of Westminster in memory of his parents, and to mark the 900th anniversary of the founding of the original Benedictine Monastery.

When we last visited Chester Cathedral we walked on the new nave flooring of Scottish sandstone, which has replaced the ancient and hence badly worn flagstones. Also comparatively new is the

Chester Cathedral. Bill Slater

vibrant, striking west window, installed in 1961. This portrays the Holy Family, St. Werburgh and several other saints.

The cloisters were originally Norman, but were rebuilt in the sixteenth century. What makes them so interesting are the small stained glass windows on all four sides, depicting the saints in the Christian calendar. The glass was installed between 1921 and 1927 and many windows bear dedications to war heroes and other prominent people. What a wonderful display they make.

In 1975 the Cathedral bells were re-hung in a new tower built next to the Memorial garden. Another modern feature at Chester will be the construction of a Song School for choristers on the old Chapter House site.

Eastgate, Chester, showing the famous clock on the City Walls bridge. Bill Slater

Chester Cathedral still has its consistory court room, the only complete example of such an ecclesiastical courtroom in England. The room is a mass of dark woodwork, with a high canopied chair for the judge. The court may still be convened by the Chancellor of the diocese, if the occasion arises. In the North Transept, you can still see the oldest part of the Cathedral, a worn Norman arch and pillars, constructed circa 1092.

From April to November visitors can view a twenty-eight-minute audio visual show in the Exhibition Centre. This facility is closed on Sundays.

Opening times: 8.00 am to 6.00 pm all the year round.
Full disabled access available.

CHESTER VISITOR CENTRE
Visitors who go to Vicar's Lane to view the Roman Amphitheatre, find themselves just across the road from Chester Visitor centre. The Centre has a big screen video theatre presenting the city's history. Local crafts are on display in a Victorian street setting. There is also a café within the centre. The Roman Amphitheatre, which is believed to have accommodated some 7,000 people, is adjacent to the Roman Garden and the City Walls.

Location: Just north of River Dee and The Groves landing stages.
Opening times: Visitor Centre opens from May to October, Monday to Saturday 9.00 am to 5.00 pm. Sunday 10.00 am to 4.00 pm.
Telephone: 01244 402111.

RIVER DEE WALK, Chester.
River boat trips from the city are expensive, but if you are prepared to walk you can see the river Dee free of charge. At the waterfront south of the city centre, we crossed the river via the white suspension bridge and then walked east along the south bank. Looking across the river, one sees beautiful riverside houses clinging to the steep slope rising from the north bank, a most charming sight.

The river in summer is a frenzy of activity, with passenger launches, motor boats, people in rowing boats, canoeists, and even the occasional rowing eight in practice. The river curves round to the south eventually. After we had walked roughly one and a half miles, we left the river and crossed fields on a path, which led into the pleasant suburb of Handbridge. We then walked through the streets back to the Dee suspension bridge. A delightful circular tour of roughly two miles. Not to be missed!

The Lady Diana motor cruiser on the river Dee at Chester. Bill Slater

The river Dee at Handbridge, Chester. Bill Slater

The river Dee at Chester, showing the salmon jumps. Bill Slater

Riding the river Dee salmon jumps at Chester. Bill Slater

THE GROSVENOR MUSEUM, Chester.

This award winning museum, situated in Grosvenor Street, gives visitors a fascinating introduction to the Roman fortress of Deva, the people who lived and worked there and the buildings which made up the fortress. The visitor can explore Roman Chester with the aid of models, murals, and artefacts excavated from the site.

The museum also presents exhibitions of life in period houses, from the 1680s to the 1920s. Plus an exhibition of Chester silverware, which includes several Chester Race Cups. There are also collections of paintings of views of the city and regularly changed temporary exhibitions in special galleries.

Opening times: Monday to Saturday 10.30 am to 5.00 pm. Sunday 2.00 pm to 5.00 pm.

Telephone: 01244 402008.

Partial disabled access only.

THE ROWS, Chester.

Chester city centre must have more magnificent black and white timber fronted buildings than any other place in Britain. The famous Rows, in Bridge Street, Eastgate Street and Watergate Street are a window shopper's delight. These upmarket shopping galleries, with their elevated covered walkways open to the streets, are thought to have gradually come into being from the Middle Ages onwards. They are unique to Chester, and are just one of the many outstanding features which make this city perhaps the most fascinating in the entire north west region.

CHESTER CITY WALLS

If you are seeking a bird's eye view of the city centre of Chester, away from the madding crowds in the streets, then the impressive City Walls walk is the answer. This stroll of just under two miles, which eventually brings you back to your starting point, takes the tourist past the many glories of Chester, in turn overlooking the Cathedral, the Rows, the river Dee and its multiplicity of pleasure craft and the Roman Amphitheatre.

It is a flat, well-paved and safe walk, with spectacular views across the surrounding countryside, as the walls are very high in some places, with several historic lookout towers to further heighten the interest. Only on the Chester Racecourse side is one briefly reduced to walking at road level.

Originally built by the Romans, the walls were strengthened and extended, long after the Romans had left Britain, by Alfred the

Great's daughter Aethelflaeda, who drove out Viking invaders. The 20th Roman Legion, conquerors of the warrior Queen Boadicea, founded Chester, or Fortress Deva (named after the River Dee), to repel Welsh tribes. The Romans had the advantage of a large inland harbour in the bowl, which is now Chester racecourse. Chester eventually lost the harbour as the river silted up.

CHESHIRE WORKSHOPS, Burwardsley, near Chester.

Fabulous displays of the candle makers' art have made this craft centre famous. It is a favourite destination for coach parties, who enjoy trips to the lovely Peckforton Hills, where the Cheshire Workshops are situated. Beeston Castle and Peckforton Castle are also situated nearby.

Demonstrations of candle making by hand are given at the Workshops (children may also have a go). There is also a restaurant.
Location: Burwardsley lies between the A49 Tarporley to Whitchurch Road, the A41 Chester to Whitchurch Road and is just west of the Peckforton Hills.
Opening times: Open daily throughout the year, 10.00 am to 5.00 pm.
Telephone: 01829 770401.
Full disabled access available.

CHRISTLETON, near Chester.

Christleton is a classic Cheshire village with lots to see, including an attractive pond area created by staff and children from the local school. There are numerous lovely buildings, including Christleton Hall (1750), Christleton House (1760), and the Old Hall (1605).

Much of the earlier village was destroyed during the Battle of Rowton Moor in 1645, a defeat for the Royalist Army which sealed the fate of King Charles. The battle site lies half a mile south of Christleton village. The presence of the Shropshire Union Canal adds extra interest to the village.
Location: The village is on A41 just half a mile east of the Broughton Hall outskirts of Chester.

DRUMLAN HALL FARM, Tattenhall, near Chester.

Drumlan Hall Farm was still admitting people free of charge at the time of writing. This traditional dairy farm of more than 300 acres is famous for home made ice cream, and visitors can select from thirty different flavours.

Children of all ages will enjoy meeting the animals, including the miniature donkeys from Sicily, which stand no more than three feet

A young visitor meets two of the goats at Drumlan Hall Farm, Tattenhall, near Chester.

high. There are also pigs, goats, sheep, rabbits, birds of prey and of course cows. Milking can be watched from a viewing platform between 1.30 pm and 3.00 pm. There is also a tea room.

Location: Drumlan Hall, Newton Lane, near Tattenhall. Two miles east of A41, and seven miles south east of Chester.

Opening times: 10.00 am to 5.30 pm, seven days a week. Winter: 10.30 am to 5.30 pm.

Telephone: 01829 770995.

Full disabled access available.

CHESHIRE HERBS near Tarporley.

At this sizeable nursery and display garden they grow more than 200 varieties of herbs. Gold medal winners at Chelsea Flower Show 1990-1999. Gift shop.

Location: On A49 trunk road between Tarporley and Sandiway.

Opening times: 10.00 am to 5.00 pm every day.

Telephone: 01829 760578.

Clitheroe

THE TOWN

The one thing you should do when visiting the ancient market town of Clitheroe, is climb the steep steps leading to the ramparts of Clitheroe Castle. The great Norman keep, dating from 1180, the only part of the original castle remaining, is perched high on a rock overlooking the town. From the top of this prominence there is a marvellous view of the famous Pendle Hill (1827 ft) which dominates Clitheroe.

Below the castle are sixteen acres of gardens and sports facilities and beyond this, the impressive river Ribble flows, giving a focus for the many riverside walks in the Clitheroe area. Beside the river, in Brungerley Park, is a series of striking sculptures which give the name to the Ribble Valley Sculpture Trail.

In 1994, the freight only branch railway line from Blackburn to Clitheroe, previously a victim of the infamous Beeching axe, was once more re-opened to passenger train traffic. The town celebrated by opening the Platform Gallery, at Clitheroe station. This art gallery also plays host to contemporary craft exhibitions by artists working in the north west. The transformation of Clitheroe station recently won a prestigious national heritage award.

Also of interest to visitors are Clitheroe's markets on Tuesdays, Thursdays and Saturdays throughout the year (Clitheroe's markets' charter dates from 1283). The town has a good museum in the Castle grounds, but there is an admission charge.

Clitheroe is a wonderful centre for exploring the many delightful villages in and around the Ribble Valley. Not far away are Downham, Waddington, Chatburn, Whitewell and Chipping. What a lovely area this is!

SAWLEY VILLAGE AND SAWLEY ABBEY, near Clitheroe

Visitors to Sawley village, situated beside the river Ribble, mainly come to see the ruins of Sawley Abbey. This was a Cistercian Abbey founded in 1147. The ruins comprise low walling and stonework at ground level, and are of limited interest to the casual observer. However Sawley itself is a lovely place.

Location: Approximately four miles north of Clitheroe, to the left of the A59 between Clitheroe and Gisburn.

WADDINGTON

Clitheroe and Pendle Hill are surrounded by those beautiful stone-built villages which make this part of Lancashire so delightful. Of these, Waddington has a unique feature in its Coronation Gardens, which border a brook in the main street. The public gardens were created to mark the Coronation of our present Queen.

The fifteenth century Waddington Old Hall has a magnificent Great Hall. Because of recent county boundary changes, Waddington was uniquely able to win the title of 'Best Kept Village in Yorkshire', and later, on several occasions, 'Best Kept Village in Lancashire'. Waddington, with its three pubs, is a large and beautiful village.

Location: Waddington is on the B6478, 1½ miles north west of Clitheroe.

DOWNHAM

This lovely place nestles amid spectacular scenery at the foot of Pendle Hill, from which a stream flows through the village. Downham was the setting for the memorable film, *Whistle Down the Wind,* starring a then teenage Hayley Mills.

Location: Downham is two miles north of Clitheroe, just off to the right of the A59, heading towards Skipton.

WHALLEY

There is an admission charge to the ruins of Whalley Abbey. But even if you do not view it, Whalley village is well worth visiting. Next to the Abbey is the fascinating thirteenth century Parish Church of St Mary and All Saints, which is usually open to the public. The superb choir stalls were originally carved for and installed in Whalley Abbey during the fifteenth century, but were moved to the Parish Church following the Dissolution of the Monasteries. There are a number of interesting memorials in the churchyard.

Whalley is situated on the B6246, just south of the point where the A59 and the A671 meet. Junction 8 off M65 and north on the A671.

Congleton

CONGLETON TOWN

One of the charms of Congleton, set in a river valley in the southeast corner of Cheshire, is that it has a small town centre 'body' and 'arms' which lead you up between the folds in the hills. The tourist can explore a town centre, which is generally lightly used by motor traffic, due to the presence of two by-pass roads around the town.

Interesting buildings include quaint pubs like the *King's Arms* and *White Lion*, plus the striking Town Hall in Venetian Gothic, bearing worn stone figures of the famous.

The local Tourist Information Centre is situated in the Town Hall.

The triangular Congleton Park is very beautiful, thanks to it being bordered on two sides by the wide river Dane and on the third by a high, wooded hill. Two footbridges cross the river, providing access

The ancient timbered King's Arms pub in Congleton town centre. It dates from 1585.

across the river to the park. At the western end of town is Astbury Mere Country Park, which provides a walk around a lake.

The town itself is limited in its visual attractions, but the hill country to the east of Congleton is quite breathtakingly beautiful, with The Cloud, a dramatic hill, dominating everything. Congleton has a delightfully old-fashioned independent newspaper, the *Congleton Chronicle*, which is worth buying to get the flavour of the place.

Congleton Museum: A town museum may be set up in 2002, behind the Town Hall.

THE CLOUD, near Congleton

The Cloud is a dramatic ridge which ends in a precipitous drop to the beginning of the Cheshire Plain around the town of Congleton. There is a strenuous but delightful walk to the summit from Timbersbrook, an attractive village which stands in an elevated position, but at the base of the ridge proper. When you get to the summit of The Cloud (343 metres high, or well in excess of 1,100 feet) you are rewarded with a stupendous view of Cheshire to the north and west, and an equally dramatic panoramic view of the hilly border of East Cheshire and North Staffordshire.

If you fancy the challenge, leave your car in the car park at Timbersbrook. From here, walk up Gosberry Hill to woodland. Carry on up through the wood to an area of heather, and thence to the surveyors trig point at the summit. The walk is nearly two miles. There is a longer alternative walk back to Timbersbrook.

Much of the land here is owned by the National Trust.

CHURCH FARM CRAFT CENTRE, Marton

This small craft centre on the A34 at Marton village, near Congleton, includes glass blowing, hand made oak furniture, antiques, artificial and dried flowers. Home-made ice cream is also available and there are farm animals on view. There is an excellent cafe serving meals.
Opening times: Open seven days a week (times vary).

Next door to Church Farm stands one of Cheshire's architectural gems, Marton Parish Church, which is claimed to be the oldest wood and plaster church still in use in Europe. This medieval black and white half-timbered building, founded in 1343, is usually open to the public. The quaint interior is kept in immaculate condition.
Location: Two miles north of Congleton on A34.

Marton Parish Church, near Congleton.

REDESMERE, near Congleton

This beautiful 1¹/₂ mile long lake is near the village of Siddington, mid-way between Alderley Edge and Congleton. It is a popular spot for afternoon visitors, who can watch the yachting and feed the large flocks of water fowl in the lovely tree-fringed surroundings. There is a footpath through the trees and along one side of the lake.

Each summer a schoolgirl is crowned queen here after a journey across the lake in a boat made to look like a swan.

Location: Redesmere is just off the A34, south of its junction with the Macclesfield to Knutsford road. (A537).

GOOSTREY, near Holmes Chapel

There is plenty to see on a walk through Goostrey, because of the size of the mile-long village. It is a mixture of old properties and modern suburbia. The Parish church of St. Luke's possesses lovely stained glass windows. We dined at the nearby *Red Lion,* a traditional and well appointed hostelry with low ceilings, impressive woodwork and good food. Afterwards we walked to the local stream and thence on a path through The Bongs, a woodland area, which leads to the former mill, now a private house. From here a road takes you back to the village centre, emerging at Main Road.

Location: Goostrey lies due south of Knutsford and north of Holmes Chapel, between the A50 and the A535.

WELLTROUGH DRIED FLOWERS, Lower Withington

Welltrough Hall Farm is a paradise for those interested in flower arranging. Farm outbuildings, including a former piggery, have been turned into eight showrooms packed with dried, silk and paper flowers, plus ceramics and other articles. This is a very colourful place to cheer oneself up in the dark midwinter! No catering was available at the time of writing, but there is a local pub which serves lunchtime meals in Lower Withington village.

Location: Lower Withington is on the B5392, one mile east of the A535 Alderley Edge to Holmes Chapel road.

Opening times: Monday to Friday 9.00 am to 5.00 pm. Saturday and Sunday 10.00 am to 5.00 pm.

Telephone: 01477 571616.

Full disabled access available.

MOW COP, near Biddulph, North Staffordshire

Mow Cop village, south of Congleton, is perched in spectacular fashion atop a 1,100 ft high ridge, which separates Cheshire and Staffordshire. Drivers can reach the village from either side and this large village is built around a gritstone crag, surmounted by Mow Cop Castle, a folly built in 1754 by a local landowner, to improve the view from his house. Paths lead up to this striking edifice, and nearby is The Old Man of Mow, a tall pillar of rock.

Mow Cop is famous as being the scene of the open-air prayer meetings held by the first Primitive Methodists.

This free day out with a difference is completed with marvellous views of the Cheshire plain and the Biddulph valley. Stand up here and you will appreciate what the villagers have to put up with in the shape of awful weather in winter. They must be a tough lot! However, you can take refuge in the local pub and enjoy a meal if you wish.

Location: Mow Cop is one mile west of Biddulph and three miles south of Congleton, between the A34 and the A527.

BRERETON COUNTRY PARK, near Congleton

Brereton Country Park consists of a fifteen-acre magnificent lake surrounded by fifty acres of hilly woodland, and two acres of heath land.

The Brimstone Trail, which leads through the woods, is extremeley interesting because of the various artists that have made unusual sculptures, which have been placed along the path. The sculptures are made of willow or hazel poles. There are animals, a giant igloo and many abstract pieces.

The Brimstone Trail is so named because this country park is the most important breeding site in Cheshire for the white and yellow Brimstone butterfly.

Activity on the lake consists of windsurfing and canoeing.

Location: Brereton Country Park, two miles from Congleton, lies on the south side of the A54 Holmes Chapel road.

Opening times: The Visitor centre, normally open seven days a week (dawn to dusk), mounts changing displays.

DUKES OAK GALLERY, Brereton Green, near Sandbach

A barn at the village of Brereton Green, has been transformed into a small gallery for contemporary art. There are also selections of sculptures, some by local artists from the area, in the gardens. Peacocks and geese roam here in a rural and rustic setting. There is also a cafe.

Location: One mile from Junction 17 of M6 towards Holmes Chapel.

Opening times: Tuesday to Friday 10.30 am to 5.00 pm. Saturday and Sunday 12.30 pm to 4.00 pm.

Telephone: 02477 532337.

Full disabled access available.

ASTBURY MEADOW GARDEN CENTRE,
near Congleton

This is a medium-sized garden centre, with extensive showrooms under glass.

Location: On A34 Newcastle Road, just south of Astbury Village.

Opening times: Open all year round, Monday to Saturday 9.00 am to 5.00 pm. Sunday 10.00 am to 5.00 pm.

Telephone: 01260 276466.

Full disabled access available.

Astbury village also boasts a magnificent village church.

The famous Saxon Crosses dominate the cobbled square at Sandbach, near Crewe.

SANDBACH

Sandbach, which is part of the Borough of Congleton, is an ancient country town famous for its enormous Saxon crosses. The two tall columns, bearing the marks of sculptors of long ago, dominate a picturesque cobbled square, which features three quaint old pubs. Nearby is the impressive St Mary's Parish Church.

Sandbach is surrounded by lovely countryside, and Congleton Council has produced a leaflet about a five-and-a-half mile walk from Sandbach town centre to the Trent and Mersey Canal and back.

Crewe and Nantwich

NANTWICH

You do not have to exert a great deal of effort to have an interesting day out in Nantwich. It is a delight to walk round the town centre and see the tremendous number of black and white timber façades of the shops and other Tudor buildings. The town is second only to Chester in having a wealth of historic buildings.

But Nantwich also boasts the famous medieval St Mary's Parish Church, dubbed 'The Cathedral of South Cheshire'. This is a wonderful example of fourteenth century architecture, built in local red sandstone. It also possesses exquisite choir stalls with intricate carvings. The church is open to visitors every day of the year from 9.00 am to 5.00 pm, (a rare treat in these days of vandalism and sacrilege).

The Crown Hotel at Nantwich (on right) was rebuilt in 1585 following a great fire which destroyed most of the town in 1583. Queen Elizabeth gave the town money for reconstruction. Elisabeth Rowlatt

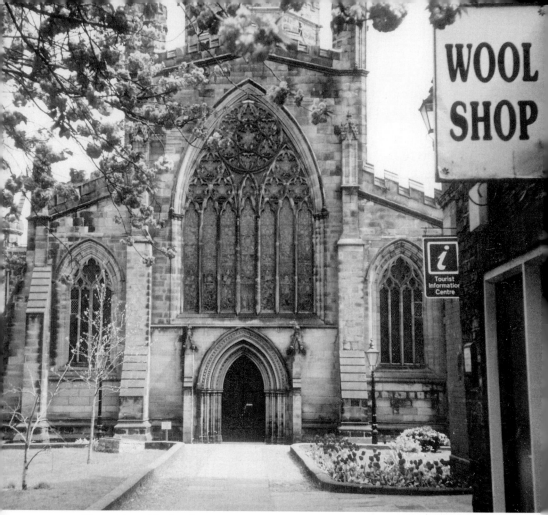

Nantwich parish church. Elisabeth Rowlatt

The free admission Nantwich Museum, which can be found in quaintly named Pillory Street, tells the history of the town and includes a Civil War display about the Battle of Nantwich. (The museum is closed on Sundays). There are also pleasant walks along the nearby river Weaver.

My wife and I enjoyed a visit to Churche's Mansion, a magnificent timber building dating from 1577, which has been restored and now serves the public as a restaurant. The building was like the coffee; black or white. The restaurant stands just outside the town centre.

QUEENS PARK, Crewe

This outstanding park was given to the people of Crewe in 1887 by the London and North Western Railway. It contains a beautiful boating lake, which is crossed at one point by a footbridge. Queens Park is well worth visiting as it possesses all the things one could ask for in a park, including beautiful trees, flower beds, sporting facilities and an aviary. The lovely park is, we suppose, one redeeming feature of this rather prosaic railway town.

Refreshments are obtainable in the pavilion.

Location: Victoria Avenue, more than a mile west of the town centre.

THE PINFOLD CRAFT CENTRE, Poole, near Nantwich

This is a purpose built craft centre containing some fifteen workshop and retail units. Crafts practised here include art, ceramics, jewellery and clothes.

There is a tea room serving snacks or full meals.

Location: On country lane that passes Cheshire College of Agriculture at Reaseheath, two miles north of Nantwich on B 5074.

Opening times: Open seven days a week from 10.00 am to 5.00 pm.

Telephone: 01270 628414.

Full disabled access available.

MUSEUM OF PRIMITIVE METHODISM, near Crewe

This free admission museum has been established in a nineteenth century chapel, at the village of Englesea Brook. A video presentation tells the story of Primitive Methodism and Englesea Brook Chapel, constructed in 1828. There is a collection of Staffordshire pottery on display. Coffee and tea are served in the museum.

Location: Just west of Junction 16 of the M6.

Opening times: Thursday, Friday, Saturday and Bank Holiday Mondays, 10.30 am to 5.30 pm. Sundays from Easter to the end of September only, 12.00 pm to 5.30 pm.

Full disabled access available.

BRIDGEMERE GARDEN WORLD, near Nantwich

This garden centre covers twenty-five acres and boasts a vast array of plants, including some which have been developed exclusively by the Bridgemere Garden World staff. There is now free admission to the entire site, including the twenty-plus themed gardens comprising 'Garden Kingdom', which includes the Television Garden seen in *Gardeners Diary*.

The rest of the centre features a huge country store, greenhouses, and an aquatics house.

There is a restaurant and coffee shop on the site.

One of the superb gardens at Bridgemere Garden World, near Nantwich. Chris Moulton

Location: On A51 seven miles southeast of Nantwich. The nearest M6 junctions are 15 and 16.
Opening times: Daily all year round, until 8.00 pm in summer, 5.00 pm in winter.
Telephone: 01270 521100.
Full disabled access available.

STAPELEY WATER GARDENS, near Nantwich
Sprawling over sixty-four acres, Stapeley Water Gardens draws 1 1/2 million visitors a year. The Water Gardens section consists of a lily covered lake and a dozen ponds. Stapeley is home to the National Collection of Nymphaea, and claims to grow more than 350 varieties of water lily.

Stapeley's free admission feature also include a pets' centre, cold water and tropical fish aquariums, aquatic plants and a new angling centre. There is however, a substantial admission charge, to 'The Palms Tropical Oasis', a spectacular indoor aquatic centre with dramatic fountains, cascades and tropical lily pools, plus giant fish and a small zoo.

There is a tea room in the garden centre and a restaurant in the Tropical Oasis.

Location: One mile south of Nantwich, on the A51 to Stone. Signposted from Junction 16 on the M6.

Opening times: Open seven days a week throughout the year. Monday to Friday 9.00 am to 5.00 pm. Saturday 10.00 am to 4.00 pm. Sunday 11.00 am to 4.00 pm.

Telephone: 01270 624188.

Full disabled access available.

DAGFIELDS CRAFTS AND ANTIQUES CENTRE, near Nantwich

Collectors of antiques will love this centre at Dagfields Farm, which boasts three large antique showrooms with a total of well in excess of 100 dealers normally in attendance. In the crafts centre there are twenty-five units, which offer, among other delights, leather goods, a candle workshop, dolls house makers, furniture, paintings, tapestries and dried flowers.

There is both a tea room and a restaurant.

Animal Village, to which there is a small admission charge, keeps the children interested with a comprehensive range of farmyard creatures.

Location: At Walgherton, three miles south east of Nantwich, near the Junction of the A51 and the B5071.

Opening times: The Dagfields farm complex is open seven days a week throughout the year, from 10.00 am to 5.30 pm.

Telephone: 01270 841336.

Full disabled access available.

Frodsham

CASTLE ARTS CENTRE, Frodsham

This Arts Centre is a credit to the people of Frodsham, for it is run and staffed by local volunteers. Opened in 1986, the arts centre occupies a restored stable block and clock tower which is part of a Victorian house, the remainder of which is now used as council offices.

Situated in the lovely surroundings of Castle Park, the arts centre has three galleries, two craft rooms and display areas for touring exhibitions and the work of local artists. The local history exhibition which is usually on permanent display, had been replaced by a photographic exhibition with an African theme when we visited, much to our disappointment. However, the coffee served to me in the gift shop was delicious.

Castle Park, Frodsham, with the tower of the arts centre on the left. Ted Birch

Walkers on crag high above Frodsham. Kath Hodgson

Location: Castle Park is on the main road through Frodsham (A56). The nearest junction on the M56 is junction 12.
Opening times: Tuesday to Saturday 10.00 am to 12.30 pm and 2.00 pm to 4.30 pm. Sunday 2.00 pm to 4.30pm.
Telephone: 01928 735832.
No specific disabled access.

The small town of Frodsham possesses an attractive centre, which is well worth visiting.

Walking: The National Trust owns land on the hill above Frodsham, and on top of the nearby towering Helsby Hill. Excellent footpaths on the tops reward the walker with spectacular views over the Mersey estuary.

Knutsford and Wilmslow

KNUTSFORD

Mrs. Gaskell, Knutsford's famous daughter, author of the novel 'Cranford' and other excellent books, died in 1865 and was buried in the churchyard of Brook Street Unitarian Chapel, the oldest place of worship in Knutsford still in use. Had she been around today, Mrs Gaskell would surely have been delighted that her beloved home town has retained much of its original character, unlike so many other towns where this has been swept away by modernisation.

Knutsford's gem, King Street, is still a narrow one-way shopping centre, cars being obliged to move between locals and tourists at a snail's pace. King Street is a delightful jumble of Georgian and many other styles of architecture. During our visit, we had coffee in one of King Street's many cafes, from the ceiling of which hung rows of penny-farthing and other types of antique bicycles.

The architectural styles in Knutsford range from half-timbered pubs to striking Italianate-style buildings erected by Richard Harding Watt, a Manchester businessman who brought a Mediterranean touch to the town in the late nineteenth century.

Knutsford Heritage Centre occupies a reconstructed seventeenth century timber framed building in King Street. Here we obtained a Town Trail guide, describing nineteen places of interest within the immediate area. Among them is Heathwaite House, in Gaskell Avenue, where as a child Mrs Gaskell lived with her aunt. The author was married in 1832, at the Georgian Parish Church of St John the Baptist.

The Parish Church at Mobberley, near Knutsford. Kath Hodgson

The highlight of Knutsford's year is the first Saturday in May, with the Royal May Day procession through the town, followed by the crowning of the May Queen and a big funfair on The Heath. All the floats and carriages in the procession are horse drawn. We have been drawn back to this charming spectacle on several occasions.

Opening times: Heritage Centre - Tuesday to Friday 1.30 pm to 4.00 pm. Saturday noon to 4.00 pm. Sunday 2.00 pm to 4.00 pm. Closed Monday.

Telephone: 01565 650506.

ROSTHERNE VILLAGE

The thatched cottages and splendid Parish Church make this village north of Knutsford a delight. A seat outside the back of the Church gives a wonderful view of Rostherne Mere far below. The Mere is a wild life sanctuary. In the church yard is the grave of George Duncan, who won the Open Golf Championship in 1920. He was a Scot who was the professional at a golf club near Knutsford.

The village is only small but it has a cricket ground next to the Church.

Location: One mile east of the A556 Altrincham to Northwich road.

Rostherne Parish Church, near Knutsford. Ken Matthews

STYAL COUNTRY PARK, near Wilmslow

Styal Country Park is centred upon the narrow valley of the river Bollin, and the cotton mill which Samuel Greg built in this beautiful setting in 1784. The mill beside the Bollin was designed to blend into the environment rather than damage it. Later, Greg also built a model village for the workers who he imported to this rural paradise. The village is well worth a visit and with this as a start point, visitors can walk down to the river through Styal Woods and then downstream along the river bank for a mile to the large hotel on the A538 Altrincham road.

The well-known walk upstream from Quarry Bank Mill, with its weir and pool, leads to lovely riverside parkland near Wilmslow called The Carrs. These river walks at Styal in the narrow ribbon of a valley are excellent in winter, as the valley walls protect the area from icy winter winds.

There is a substantial admission charge to Quarry Bank Mill, which is an excellent textile museum. There is however, a separate entrance to the basement restaurant. Styal has been a tourist mecca since 1939, when the mill owners gave mill, village, farms and surrounding woodland to the National Trust. Production at the mill ceased in 1959 and in 1979 the building was re-opened as a museum.

One prize exhibit at Styal is the tree that stands inside the

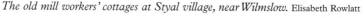

The old mill workers' cottages at Styal village, near Wilmslow. Elisabeth Rowlatt

The old Co-op shop at Styal village, near Wilmslow. Elisabeth Rowlatt

boundary line at Styal Cricket Club. This author once took part in a last wicket stand here and one of my shots saw the ball hit this tree. As was customary, I was awarded four runs, although the ball did not actually reach the boundary.

Location: Styal is on the B5166 Wilmslow to Gatley road.

ALDERLEY EDGE, near Wilmslow

One of the most popular day trip destinations in the north west, the Edge rears abruptly from the Cheshire plain, sporting outcrops of sandstone to walk over. The Edge, approached by road from the south end of Alderley Edge village, is covered with huge trees, mainly beech and pine, leaving the walker feeling as if they are walking in an open air cathedral. The trees also protect winter visitors from icy winds, and in summer from the heat.

This National Trust property was once noted for its copper mines, evidence of which is still to be seen. Now the mansions of the wealthy demonstrate how Alderley Edge sprang up as a commuter centre, following the arrival of the railway. From the top of the Edge there is a wonderful panoramic view towards Manchester. Fast and frequent trains run from Manchester to Alderley Edge.

Location: On B5087 Alderley to Macclesfield Road.

TATTON PARK, near Knutsford

Tatton Park is a vast deer park containing large herds of fallow and red deer. There are also a great many sheep. The park is 2¹/₂ miles long from north to south and almost two miles across, at its widest point.

The famous Tatton Mere is almost a mile long and is used for boating and sail boarding and offers bathing from a sandy beach on the east bank. Because of the park's size, bicycles are available for hire at Tatton Hall.

Visitors must pay a substantial entrance fee for cars to enter the park, so if possible, leave your car outside the Knutsford entrance to avoid undue expense. You cannot park outside the Rostherne entrance because of double yellow lines in the lanes there.

There are separate admission charges for Tatton Hall, the lovely gardens and the medieval Old Hall. There is an excellent restaurant in the courtyard outside Tatton Hall.

Location: Tatton Park's southern point is adjacent to Knutsford town. It lies just east of the A556 Manchester to Chester road.

Opening times: Tuesday to Sunday, 10.00 am to 7.00 pm.

Telephone: 01625 534400.

AVIATION VIEWING PARK, MANCHESTER AIRPORT

This excellent viewing park for plane spotters of all ages is situated near the southern end of the runways. It is near junction 6 of the M56, from where you drive a short distance along the A538 towards Wilmslow, before turning left up Sunbank Lane to *The Romper* public house. A lane on the right here leads to a pay cabin at the viewing park. I include this attraction in this book because the admission charges amount to no more than a normal car parking charge, and you can stay here all day if you wish.

The viewing park features three viewing platforms which are on top of high grassed mounds. At busy periods aircraft take off or land every minute or two, so it is a great show. Aircraft take off past the viewing platforms, and planes landing turn round and taxi past the viewing park. Viewing park facilities include a small visitor centre, an aviation shop selling all kinds of models, a mobile snack bar and toilets.

Hot meals are available at the delightful *Romper* pub nearby.

Charges: car and driver £1.50 Monday to Friday, £2.50 Saturday, Sunday and Bank Holidays. Car passengers 50p each. Children up to the age of sixteen years of age go free.

Location: Off Altrincham Road, Ringway.

Opening times: 8.30 am to dusk, according to time of year.

Telephone: 01625 534790.

Lancaster

LANCASTER CITY CENTRE WALK

Those who holiday at Morecambe have more than a seaside resort to explore, for nearby Lancaster is an historical and architectural gem. An excellent place to commence any city walk is at the Tourist Information Centre at Castle Hill. This was the site of a Roman military headquarters, and at Vicarage Lane you can see the remains of a Roman bath house. This attraction has free access.

Lancaster's grim Norman castle is still used as a prison to this day. Nearby is the splendid Priory Church. Vicarage Lane leads down to the river Lune and the interesting St George's Quay, with the former Custom House, warehouses and pubs reminding us of Lancaster's importance as a port during the eighteenth century.

The city centre boasts numerous impressive buildings, many of them Georgian. These include the Judges' Lodgings, the Old Town Hall, the Music Room, Penny's Hospital almshouses, and the imposing Town Hall built in 1909 (now the City Museum).

LANCASTER CITY MUSEUM

The City Museum is housed in the former Town Hall, an impressive pile faced with huge columns. It was built in 1871-3 in the city centre. In 2001 there was a proposal to close the Museum as a council economy measure. Fortunately the proposal was rejected and the city museum will stay open, presumably still as a free admission place.

The Museum was founded in 1923, and its collections illustrate the history and archaeology of Lancaster and also covers the most northerly and rural parts of Lancashire.

In the same building (free admission) is the King's Own Museum. The King's Own Royal Regiment (4th Foot) was raised in 1680 and saw service all over the world from Tangier to Ethiopia, from the West Indies to the Western Front. This Museum has recently been re-displayed.

Location: Market Square.
Opening times: Monday to Saturday 10.00 am to 5.00 pm.
Telephone: 01524 64637.
Full disabled access available.

STOREY ART GALLERY, Lancaster
This two-room gallery is run by local artists.
Location: Meeting House Lane, just south of Lancaster Castle.
Opening times: Monday to Saturday, 9.00 am to 4.00 pm.
Telephone: 01524 849494.
Partial disabled access only.

ASHTON MEMORIAL, Williamson Park, Lancaster
Many drivers whizzing past Lancaster on the M6, as they head north
to the Cumbrian Lakes, must be intrigued by the striking building in
white Portland stone which they see above them, high on a hill.
Resembling the top tiers of some fantastic wedding cake, this is a
place which perhaps many feel they would like to visit one day. The
building is in fact the Ashton Memorial, which is indeed open to the
public all throughout the year.

Inside it consists of two large domed chambers, one above the
other. There are also several external balconies, giving visitors
fabulous views over the rooftops of Lancaster, across the river
Lune to Morecambe Bay, and across miles of countryside.
Exhibitions of works of art and photography are held regularly in
the Ashton Memorial.

Williamson Park, in which it stands, features a tropical butterfly
house, for which there is an admission charge. Admission is free to
the ground floor exhibition at the Ashton Memorial, but there is a
charge for the first floor exhibition.

The Ashton Memorial, which was erected between 1907 and
1909, by Lord Ashton, stands as a memorial to his family, or as
some would have it, to his wife. Lord Ashton's father was the
Lancaster oilcloth and linoleum tycoon James Williamson, who in
1877 bought quarry rights on this hill and created the forty-acre
Williamson Park, entirely at his own expense. He and his sons
fashioned rock gardens, an ornamental lake, plus an eighty-foot high
cascade.
Location: Wyresdale Road, one mile east of Lancaster city centre.
Opening times:
  Easter to September, every day of the week from 10.00 am to
  5.00 pm.
  October to Easter, Monday to Friday, 11.00 am to 4.00 pm.
  Saturday, Sunday, 10.00 am to 4.00 pm.
Telephone: 01524 33318.
Partial disabled access only at Ashton Memorial.

The Ashton Memorial in Williamson Park, Lancaster. John Moorhouse

LANCASTER PRIORY AND PARISH CHURCH, Castle Hill

The ancient Priory Church of Lancaster shares its elevated position on Castle Hill with Lancaster Castle (admission charge to the Castle). The Priory Church, founded as a monastery by Roger de Poitou in 1094, on the site of an earlier Saxon church, is open to the public throughout the year.

Lancaster Priory Church. John Moorhouse

Its lovely interior, much of it medieval, includes brilliantly carved choir stalls and The King's Own Memorial Chapel. Much of the church is thirteenth century, but the tower was rebuilt in 1755. **Telephone:** 01524 65338.

ST. PETER'S CATHEDRAL, East Road, Lancaster

The impressive interior of Lancaster's Roman Catholic Cathedral has undergone a brilliant renovation in recent years, which is well worth seeing. The Cathedral has an unusually tall spire, which rises to 240 ft. Although built in 1859, it was designed after the style of the 1300s, by Lancaster architect Edward Paley.
Telephone: 01524 61860.

LANCASTER UNIVERSITY GALLERIES

The Peter Scott Gallery is Lancaster University's main art gallery. It is an unusual building, having been created by roofing in a previously open courtyard, which was surrounded by existing university buildings.

The gallery's main collections include twentieth century art by British, European, Chinese and Japanese artists. The upstairs section features contemporary pottery and also Royal Lancastrian pottery, made at Clifton Junction, Salford. There is much to see here, but the gallery is most likely to be closed during university holidays, so it is advisable to telephone to check first.

There is a coffee bar outside the building.
Opening times: Monday to Friday, noon to 5.00 pm. Closed Saturday and Sunday.
Telephone: 01524 593057.

Also within the University campus area and only five minutes' walk away, is the Ruskin Library, which possesses a small art gallery used for temporary exhibitions. It is a circular building opened in 1997 and is well worth a visit.
Location: Lancaster University Galleries are on the A6 one mile south of the city centre, so there are no parking problems.
To avoid city centre traffic, leave the M6 at Junction 33.
Full disabled access available.

WOLF HOUSE GALLERY, Gibraltar, Silverdale, near Carnforth

Converted Georgian farm buildings provide a craft and art centre here. The main gallery is a former cow shippon, which now has on display, collections of ceramics, toys and glass. The former dairy now contains displays of knitwear, while across the courtyard the old coach house contains paintings and wooden rocking horses.
There is an adventure play area for children.
Location: Silverdale is on the coast between Arnside and Carnforth. Leave M6 at junction 35.

Opening times:
  From Easter to Christmas Eve, Tuesdays to Saturdays, 10.30 am
  to 1.00 pm and 2.00 pm to 5.30 pm.
  From January to Easter, Open Saturdays and Sundays.
Telephone: 01524 701405.
Full disabled access available.

HEYSHAM VILLAGE, Morecambe

The ancient village of Heysham can be visited by riding across the
sands on the regular service from Morecambe, in a trailer drawn by
a tractor. Heysham is an attractive village with several cafes where
meals or snacks are available.

St Peter's Church was founded in approximately 967 A.D. and is
one of the oldest churches still in regular use in Europe. On a hill-top
nearby, stand the ruins of St Patrick's Chapel, which is even older
than St Peter's and is said to have been built by St Patrick, patron
saint of Ireland. If this is correct, the structure dates from somewhere
in the fifth century A.D.

The present Heysham harbour was opened in 1904. Prior to this
new harbour being opened, there were many shipwrecks in the
approaches to Heysham and on occasion, some of these wrecks can
still be seen.

HAPPY MOUNT PARK, Morecambe

Beautiful gardens are a feature of this park. Miniature railway,
paddling pool, adventure play area.
Location: Marine Road East.

Eric Morecambe's statue

Also worth seeing, on the promenade, is a statue of the Morecambe
born comedian. Gardens have been created round the statue.
Thousands of people have flocked to Morecambe just to see this
marvellous tribute to the great man.

Liverpool

LIVERPOOL CATHEDRAL

A double sightseeing treat lies in store for visitors to Liverpool with the city's two so very different great cathedrals. Standing at opposite ends of Hope Street, the Anglican and Roman Catholic edifices are sufficiently close to each other to enable the visitor to tour them both in one day.

Liverpool's Anglican Cathedral is believed to be the largest in Britain, possessing more floor space than any other. Walking around the outside of the cathedral, we felt as though we were at the foot of an enormous cliff of sandstone. The interior is so vast that one feels positively Lilliputian!

The foundation stone of this Cathedral was laid by King Edward VII, in 1904. Due to work proceeding at a slower than normal pace during the two World Wars, the construction work was not completed until 1978. Designed by Giles Gilbert Scott in a Gothic Revival style, (Scott was only twenty-two years of age when he won the competition), Liverpool Cathedral must surely be the last of the vast 'traditional' style cathedrals to be erected in Britain.

The sandstone blocks cladding the exterior are unlikely to crumble. The stone was quarried at Woolton, in south Liverpool,

Liverpool's huge Anglican cathedral. Bill Slater

An aerial vew of Liverpool Cathedral. Bill Slater

which provided the hardest sandstone available in the region. The Lady Chapel was the first part of the Cathedral to be completed in 1910, and was immediately used for religious services. The organ, the installation of which was completed in 1926, boasts 9,765 pipes and is the world's biggest. We hope that someone is playing this magnificent instrument during your visit. Among the Cathedral's treasures are the superb West End stained glass windows. The Cathedral has both the heaviest peal of bells in the world and the highest, at 200 feet above floor level.

The Cathedral's stupendous square tower is just over 331 feet high at its peak. Two lifts take visitors most of the way up, but this ride is followed by 108 steps to the top! Visitors must pay a charge for this ascent, which does provide a fabulous view of Merseyside. The tower visit fee also includes admission to an embroidery exhibition in the triforium gallery.

Other Cathedral facilities include a restaurant and Visitor Centre.

Location: St. James Mount, Hope Street.

Opening times: Cathedral 8.00 am to 6.00 pm. (5.30 pm if there is an Evensong service).

Telephone: 0151 709 6271.

Full disabled access available.

METROPOLITAN CATHEDRAL OF CHRIST THE KING

I suppose that the nickname of 'Paddy's Wigwam', given to Liverpool's Metropolitan Cathedral of Christ the King, is both amusing and appropriate. This circular Catholic Cathedral does bear a striking resemblance to an Indian tepee. It looks at its best at night when in use, as the stained glass windows in the huge central tower glow in the dark from the lights within.

The interior of the building is impressive, with the tower directly above the central High Altar. It is a glorious sight as the sunshine floods through the red and blue stained glass up there. The congregation, seated around the altar in the centre, has a wonderful view of what is going on. Services here have a special dramatic impact. The altar is a rectangular block of white marble quarried near Skopje in Yugoslavia, and is supported on a plinth of the same material.

Around the perimeter of the circular nave are various small chapels. The stained glass windows in the cathedral are of abstract design.

The cathedral was opened in 1967 and took less than five years to build. The design by Sir Frederick Gibberd, was chosen from 300 entries from many parts of the world. In typical 1960s 'tradition', it is built mainly of concrete, some 30,000 tons were used, as well as 1,500 tons of steel, 1,800 tons of stone, 700 tons of slate, 300 tons of marble and 1.5 million bricks. The cathedral's bells are housed in a ninety-foot high tower, above the main entrance.

Before the Second World War, Liverpool's Catholics had begun to construct a very different cathedral on this site. It was to be a vast edifice with a massive dome bigger even than St Peter's in Rome. They built an enormous crypt before hostilities intervened. After the war they realised that the cost of a building of traditional design would be prohibitive. As a result, the present building was erected on top of the huge crypt. The crypt entrance is some way from the cathedral and visitors can see its various chapels.

Because this cathedral is so modern in design and so unusual, it forms a perfect contrast to the Anglican Cathedral. Liverpool has a unique double tourist attraction here!

Religious note: The Catholic Cathedral's architect was in fact a Protestant, while the architect of the Anglican Cathedral was a Catholic.

Location: The main entrance to the Cathedral is between Mount Pleasant and Duckinfield Street.

Opening times: 8.00 am to 6.00 pm daily. Tea shop in Cathedral.

Telephone: 0151 709 9222.

Full disabled access available.

A Mersey ferry passes the Liverpool waterfront. Heather Bradshaw

A corner of the Albert Dock shops and leisure area, Liverpool. Bill Slater

ALBERT DOCK, Liverpool

The vast former warehouse complex of Liverpool's Albert Dock area, which was constructed in the mid-nineteenth century, has now been converted into one of Britain's most popular attractions. The visitor is free to walk round scores of speciality shops, or call in at bars, restaurants and cafes. It is a stunning quayside location with fine views across the Mersey from the riverside walk. As the readily available leaflet we collected advised us: 'Your quay to a great day out'.

Here is the Tate Gallery of modern art, the large Merseyside Maritime Museum, which also contains HM Customs and Excise National Museum, plus The Beatles Story centre, with the Museum of Liverpool Life at nearby Canning Dock.

There is a vast free car park and free admission to Albert Dock, which in its restored warehouses boasts the largest group of Grade One listed buildings in Britain.

Albert Dock was a part of the 7^1/$_2$ miles of docks and warehouses that made Liverpool the world's greatest port. The first 'wet dock' in Liverpool was built in 1715. The early wealth of Liverpool was based on the slave trade. At one time the city docks were home port to more than 100 ships engaged in the transport of Africans to the slave markets of America. When slavery was abolished in 1807, Liverpool then turned to the importation of cotton from America. Albert Dock's five-storey warehouses were built next to the water so that cargoes could be transferred straight from ships to storage. However, during the years after the Second World War, they fell into disuse, becoming derelict before the brilliant restoration job, the result of which we see today.

Location: Just south of Pier Head and the Royal Liver Building.
Opening times: Albert Dock is open seven days a week from 10.00 am.
Telephone: 0151 708 8574.
Full disabled access available.

TATE GALLERY

The Tate Gallery's North of England headquarters opened in 1988 in one of the Albert Dock's warehouses, and houses part of the National collection of Modern Art. Up to 1997 the Gallery had attracted more than five million visitors, nearly three times the number originally anticipated.

The top floor of the building has now been developed to house new galleries, following the building's closure between April 1997 and May 1998. There is also a new café, bar, auditorium and education studios. Admission to this mecca for twentieth century artists and sculptors is free, but there are charges should you wish to view special exhibitions.

Opening times: Tuesday to Sunday 10.00 am to 6.00 pm. Closed Mondays except Bank Holidays. Closed Good Friday.
Telephone: 0151 709 3223.
Full disabled access available.

OPEN EYE GALLERY, Liverpool

This is Merseyside's centre for the photographic and media arts. The programme of contemporary exhibitions by regional and national artists involves a fresh exhibition every few weeks.

Location: 280 Wood Street (midway between Albert Dock and Liverpool's two cathedrals).
Opening times: Tuesday to Friday 10.30 am to 5.30 pm. Saturday 10.30 am to 5.00 pm. Closed Sundays, Mondays and Bank Holidays.
Full disabled access available.

UNIVERSITY OF LIVERPOOL ART GALLERY

Liverpool's superlative collection of art galleries includes the University gallery, which occupies an elegant Georgian terraced house at 3, Abercrombie Square, not far from the Metropolitan Cathedral of Christ the King.

The collection of British oil paintings, watercolours, sculpture, furniture and textiles has been part of the University's history since its foundation in 1881.

Among highlights are English watercolours, paintings by Joseph Wright of Derby, Turner, and the wild-life artist John Audubon. Early English porcelain, and stained glass cartoons by Edward Burne-Jones, are also on view, along with important works by Jacob Epstein and other twentieth century artists.

Opening times: Monday, Tuesday, Thursday, 12 noon to 2.00 pm. Wednesday, Friday 12 noon to 4.00 pm. Closed weekends, Bank Holidays and throughout August.
Telephone: 0151 794 2357(8).
No specific disabled access.
Note: In nearby Senate House, Oxford Street, temporary exhibitions are held in term time. Programme includes work by contemporary artists and displays from the University Collections.

SEFTON PARK, Liverpool.

It is generally understood that outside London, Liverpool's Sefton

Park is the largest inner city park in Britain. The kidney-shaped park is one mile from north to south. Its attractions include fine woodland aspects, the huge Victorian Palm House, the boating lake, and the central glen with its river-like water areas.

This land was originally owned by the Earl of Sefton. In 1867 Liverpool Corporation bought 375 acres at a cost of £250,000 to construct a huge 'pleasure ground'. The Corporation financed development of the park by later selling some of the land for housing.

We took friends to Sefton Park at the end of May, when the rhododendrons were in bloom around the attractive water glen areas. We followed the line of pools that fill the glen in the middle of the park. The enormous circular Palm House, containing date palms and a host of other plants, was awaiting restoration work at an estimated cost of £1 million. I was told that this impressive domed structure was to be extended on one side to provide a cafe and toilets. Outside the Palm House a park ranger was about to take visitors on a walking tour of the park. In these days of country parks a new breed of ranger has arisen, complete with Land Rovers.

We spent 3¹/₂ hours in Sefton Park, finishing our visit with a delightful stroll around the massive boating lake, surrounded by wooded slopes, all of which creates a beautiful scene.

Location: Sefton Park is one mile south of the city centre, between the A561 and A562.

CALDERSTONES PARK, Liverpool

Only one mile from Sefton Park is Calderstones Park, regarded a Liverpool's best after Sefton. We toured the lovely gardens here to complete a great day out.

Location: On A562, between Childwall and Allerton.

CROXTETH COUNTRY PARK, West Derby, Liverpool

This large country park at West Derby was once the estate of the Earls of Sefton. They lived here at Croxteth Hall, a magnificent mansion now open to the public, (there is an admission charge for entry to the Hall). However, there is much to see without touring the house itself. A good time to visit Croxteth is in late May or June, when there is a marvellous display of rhododendrons and azaleas.

The gardens include a substantial walled garden and ornamental ponds. There are also various fine estate buildings to see. Home Farm is now run as a Rare Breeds Centre and there is an admission charge to this.

When the seventh Earl of Sefton died childless in 1972, his widow decided that the estate should be handed over for public use.

Location: Croxteth Country Park is on the eastern outskirts of Liverpool, one mile south of the A580 East Lancs Road, and a mile west of the M57.

Opening times: Park and Home Farm open all year round. All facilities open Easter to September (11.00 am to 5.00 pm).

Telephone: 0151 228 5311.

ROYAL LIVER BUILDING, Pier Head

Free guided tours of the famous Royal Liver Building at Liverpool Pier Head take place from April to September. Individuals or groups are welcome, but tours must be booked in advance by calling on 0151 236 2748. Tours start at 2.00 pm, Monday to Friday.

The 17-storey building was erected between 1908 and 1911 as the headquarters of the Royal Liver Assurance, and stands an impressive 322 feet to the top of the legendary Liver Birds, which perch on top of the building's two towers. The Liver Birds are eighteen feet high, and below them, on the front tower, are four clock faces, which at twenty-five feet in diameter are $2\frac{1}{2}$ feet larger than those of Big Ben in London. The clock's minute hands are fourteen feet long and the clock mechanism itself weighs four tons.

During the 1980s the building was refurbished, and decades of dirt

The Liver Building, Liverpool. Joyce Hollows

The Liver Building and the Customs House on Liverpool's waterfront. Bill Slater

and grime were sand blasted from the granite exterior. The ground floor, once the shipping centre for Liverpool passenger liners, was restored to its former glory. One half of it is now a stockbroking centre, while the other half, which is open to the public, includes a magnificent courtyard area, floored in Spanish marble and inlaid in the centre with a replica of the Royal Liver clock faces.

Opening times: Open to the public during normal business hours. Full disabled access available.

LIVERPOOL PARISH CHURCH

The Church of Our Lady and St Nicholas in Chapel Street was rebuilt in the late 1940s. The old building, largely unchanged since 1815, was destroyed by fire during a wartime air raid in 1940. Only the tower and lantern survived, and the tower, which has been incorporated into the new building, is still the most notable part of this church. The new building was constructed of Stanton stone, quarried at Macclesfield.

In 1993, Princess Alexandra opened a Parish Centre, which includes a refreshment room. The churchyard became a public garden in 1891. The church is open to the public.

MATTHEW STREET GALLERY, Liverpool

This small gallery specialises in the art of John Lennon, who studied at Liverpool Art College, where he met his first wife Cynthia, a fellow student. The fifty-odd exhibits, mainly line drawings and cartoons, are for sale. Lennon's work fetches between £400 and £5,000 (for a signed item). Also other items about the Beatles on show.

Location: Matthew Street is between Lord Street and Victoria Street, city centre.

Opening times: Monday to Saturday 10.00 am to 5.00 pm. Sunday, 11.00 am to 4.00 pm.

Telephone: 0151 236 0009.

INDIA BUILDINGS, Liverpool

Antiques gallery specialising in art noveau and art deco.

Location: Near waterfront behind Cunard building (Water Street).

Opening times: Monday to Friday 10.00 am to 6.00 pm.

Telephone: 0151 236 1282.

HERITAGE MARKET, Liverpool

Claimed to be one of the biggest markets in Britain, with up to 500 stalls set in a Victorian listed warehouse.

Location: Stanley Dock, Great Howard Street.

Opening times: Sundays 9.00 am to 4.00 pm.

Telephone: 0151 207 0441.

THE QUIGGINS CENTRE, Liverpool

An alternative shopping experience, with designer clothing and retro, antiques, furniture and hand crafted goods. Display centre and café.

Location: School Lane, Liverpool.

Opening times: Monday to Saturday 10.00 am to 6.00 pm.

Telephone: 0151 709 2462.

STANLEY DOCK SUNDAY MARKET, Liverpool

Historic indoor and outdoor market with up to 400 stalls.

Location: Horse drawn bus to the market runs from Albert Dock, one mile away. Market entrance at Great Howard Street and Regent Road.

Opening times: Open every Sunday 9.00 am to 4.00 pm.

Telephone: 0151 298 1978.

HALE, near Liverpool

Situated well away from Liverpool's southern outpost of Speke, charming Hale village is noted for its numerous thatched houses, both ancient and modern. From the village you can walk to the now disused Hale Lighthouse near the river Mersey. There is also a bird sanctuary near the village.

Each year Hale elects its own Lord Mayor from among those who have rendered service to the village In the churchyard can be seen the 1623 grave of John Middleton who, it was claimed, was nine foot three inches tall. He also features large on the village inn sign.

Location: Hale is well south of the A561 and A562 Liverpool to Widnes roads.

BLUECOAT CHAMBERS, Liverpool

Bluecoat Chambers is a striking Queen Anne building which was completed 1725 and is now the venue for a crafts centre and art gallery. There is a cobbled courtyard and a walled garden.

Until the turn of the century the famous Bluecoat School, founded for orphans and the children of seafarers, was housed here. The school then moved out to the suburbs, at Wavertree. The Bluecoat Display Centre is situated in the walled garden, and specialises in contemporary hand-made glass, ceramics, studio pottery, jewellery, wood and textiles from craft workers across Britain. The Art Gallery mounts eight exhibitions each year.

The Bluecoat Chambers also house a café, bar, local history shop, bookshop and an arts shop.

Location: School Lane, (between Littlewoods Store and Burtons).
Opening times: Monday to Saturday 10.00 am to 5.30 pm.
Art gallery closed Monday.
Telephone: 0151 709 4014. Partial disabled access only.

THE NATIONAL MUSEUMS AND ART GALLERIES ON MERSEYSIDE PASS

In 1997 eight of the major Merseyside art galleries and museums were included in a new scheme involving the purchase of a £3 pass which gives unlimited admission to them all for twelve months.

So when you pay a first visit to any of the attractions, listed below, you should obtain a twelve month NMGM pass (it is free for students, under-sixteens, pensioners and the unemployed). I have included these places in this book because the cost is negligible if one pays several visits to them in one year. And they are outstanding museums and galleries.

Included in the National Museums and Galleries on Merseyside scheme are:

Merseyside Maritime Museum
H.M. Customs and Excise National Museum
Museum of Liverpool Life
Liverpool Museum
Walker Art Gallery
Lady Lever Art Gallery
Sudley House
The Conservation Centre

All the above places can be contacted by telephoning the Merseyside Galleries and Museums on 0151 207 0001. Alternatively telephone the individual numbers given below.

Details covering these eight attractions form the last section of this Liverpool list. During the first few months of the NMGM pass scheme, there was an amazing thirty-five per cent overall increase in attendance at the eight venues. Having paid for a pass, people were obviously determined to obtain the maximum value from them.

Normally – if charges are imposed at previously free admission venues, there is a decrease in attendance. The Liverpool scheme had shown the way to other cities with their novel and popular approach.

All the above Museums and Galleries have full disabled access available with the exception of Sudley House.

THE LADY LEVER ART GALLERY, Port Sunlight, Bebbington, Wirral

Do not miss this treasure chest of Victorian paintings, English eighteenth century furniture, tapestries, sculpture, Wedgwood and Chinese porcelain. A new permanent display, 'The Making of a Gallery', shows the full collecting passion of William Hesketh Lever, who created and filled this marvellous building.

Location: From the A41 follow signs for Port Sunlight. From the M53 exit at Junction 4.

Opening times: Monday to Saturday 10.00 am to 5.00 pm. Sunday noon to 5.00 pm.

Telephone: 0151 478 4126.

Note: There is more information on Port Sunlight in the Wirral pages.

MUSEUM OF LIVERPOOL LIFE, Albert Dock

We had a pleasant surprise when visiting this interesting museum, for in it we came upon a small cinema, with plush tip-up seats. What a relief to sink into the upholstery and rest weary feet while watching a film on the big screen about the history of the Grand National steeplechase. Touring museums can be a tiring experience, especially if no seats are available, and this little cinema provided a merciful and fascinating relief.

The Museum of Liverpool Life, which stands at the quayside near Albert Dock, explores the history of Liverpool and its people. As an aside, my first car was a new Ford Anglia and the museum displays the first Anglia to come off the production line at Halewood, making me feel a trifle nostalgic.

A reminder of the privations of the working class in the days before modern semi-detached housing, is a life-size reconstruction of a Liverpool slum court, with miserable house fronts and one communal lavatory for many families. On the bright side, visitors can talk to a family from the television soap opera 'Brookside', admire Dixie Dean's medals from his days with Everton and England and operate a hand printing press.

Opening times: Open daily 10.00 am to 5.00 pm.
Telephone: 0151 478 4080.

Piermaster's House: Near the museum is the Piermaster's House of 1856, which has been restored and is open to the public.

MERSEYSIDE MARITIME MUSEUM, Albert Dock

This museum occupies five floors of a large building, and contains one of the finest maritime collections in the world. There is an impressive array of model ships, most of them made for publicity purposes, by the builders of the ships concerned. The model of the ill-fated *Titanic* is almost twenty feet long!

In the gallery featuring the transatlantic slave trade, one passes through the dark hold of a slave ship and listens to true accounts by

The waterfront at the Maritime Museum, Liverpool. David Williams

surviving slaves, of the horrific conditions aboard the slavers.

There is also an award-winning Emigrants to the New World gallery. Experience the hardships of the nine million people who sailed from Liverpool to new lands, mainly America, between 1830 and 1930.

There are excellent galleries about the Second World War at sea. On the top floor there is an excellent restaurant, with lovely views over the dockland area.

Opening times: Open daily 10.00 am to 5.00 pm.
Telephone: 0151 478 4499.

CUSTOMS MUSEUM

On the ground floor of the Maritime Museum building is the Customs and Excise National Museum. Its imaginative displays highlight aspects of Customs work, with the vital war against modern drug smuggling prominent.

Opening times: Open daily 10.00 am to 5.00 pm.
Telephone: 0151 478 4499.

PILOT CUTTER

During the summer months, visitors can pay free visits to the Liverpool pilot cutter *Edmund Gardner*, which is in dry dock near the Maritime Museum. It was the last of the big Liverpool pilot boats, built like a miniature liner.

THE CONSERVATION CENTRE, Whitechapel, Liverpool.

The Conservation Centre was set up by National Museums and Galleries on Merseyside to care for the 1.2 million objects in its collections. It is the only such centre in Europe to open its doors to the public.

The centre is housed in a former Midland Railway Goods Depot, a Grade 2 listed Victorian warehouse. Here visitors see how the experts stop paint flaking from Old Masters, or how a laser cleans time-blackened sculptures.

Location: In Whitechapel, not far from the Mersey Tunnel entrance.
Opening times: Monday to Saturday 10.00 am to 5.00 pm. Sunday 12 noon to 5.00 pm. Licensed cafe.
Telephone: 0151 478 4999.

LIVERPOOL MUSEUM AND PLANETARIUM

This brilliant museum has collections from all over the world, ranging from the wonders of the Amazonian rain forests to relics of Ancient Egypt.

A view of Liverpool and the Mersey from the air. Bill Slater

There is an award-winning Natural History Centre, Space Gallery, aquarium, vivarium and historic transport section.

There is an admission charge for the Planetarium. There are cafe and restaurant facilities.

At the time of writing the museum was being expanded into an adjacent building.

Location: William Brown Street (Near St. George's Hall).

Opening times: Monday to Saturday 10.00 am to 5.00 pm. Sunday noon to 5.00 pm.

Telephone: 0151 478 4399.

SUDLEY HOUSE, Aigburth, Liverpool

Standing in its own parkland, Sudley House dates from 1840 and was formerly the home of Victorian shipping magnate George Holt, whose brother Albert, ran a rival Liverpool shipping line. The two-storey property is filled with George Holt's fine collection of eighteenth and nineteenth century paintings, including works by Gainsborough, Millais and Turner.

This treasure house of art was bequeathed to the City of Liverpool by George Holt's daughter Emma, who died in 1944.

Location: Mossley Hill Road, Aigburth.

Opening times: Monday to Saturday 10.00 am to 5.00 pm. Sunday noon to 5.00 pm. The cafe is open at weekends and Bank Holidays.

Telephone: 0151 724 3245.

Partial disabled access only.

The Walker Art Gallery, Liverpool. David Williams

WALKER ART GALLERY, Liverpool

This magnificent classical stone building was erected with money provided by Sir Andrew Barclay Walker, who was Liverpool's mayor in 1873. It houses a wonderful collection of European art dating from 1300 to the twentieth century, which in Britain is surpassed only by certain London galleries.

There are works by Rembrandt, Van Dyck, Rubens, and Liverpool born George Stubbs. The Sculpture Gallery received a National Art Collections Award in 1989. Pre-Raphaelite and modern British art is also well represented.

The Walker Art Gallery in William Brown Street is one of several classical buildings here that make a city centre walkabout a rewarding experience. Few cities can compete with Liverpool's splendour.

The Walker Art Gallery closed in June, 2001 for improvement work to be carried out. It was opening again in the Spring of 2002,
Opening times: Monday to Saturday 10.00 am to 5.00 pm. Sunday noon to 5.00 pm. Cafe.
Telephone: 0151 478 4199

Macclesfield

WEST PARK MUSEUM, Prestbury Road, Macclesfield

West Park Museum, which is located just inside West Park, opened in 1898 and was provided for the people of Macclesfield by Marianne Brocklehurst and her brother, Peter. The museum's collection of ancient Egyptian artefacts was acquired by Marianne Brocklehurst during several visits to Egypt.

Also on view are local history items and works of art, including the work of famous bird artist Charles Tunnicliffe, born locally at Langley.

Opening times: Tuesday to Sunday, 1.30 pm to 4.30 pm. Closed Mondays.

Telephone: 01625 619831.

Full disabled access available.

TEGG'S NOSE COUNTRY PARK, near Macclesfield

This country park occupies the high ridge known as Tegg's Nose, once the location of several stone quarries and, therefore, littered with rocks and rock faces.

From the high walks in this small country park, there are wonderful views across moorland to Macclesfield Forest, and of the Cheshire Plain to the southwest. A display of quarrying tools, machinery and products is on view at the Park Centre.

There is a refreshment kiosk.

Location: Just south of the A537 Macclesfield to Buxton road and 1 1/2 miles east of Macclesfield.

Opening times: Dawn to dusk.

PRESTBURY, near Macclesfield

Prestbury is a Rolls Royce of a village and there are a great many Roller owners living in this affluent commuter centre near Macclesfield.

At weekends, many visitors are to be found parading along the main street, with its pleasing shops, black and white timber bank, Prestbury Hall and the ancient Legh Arms, which dates from 1580.

Overlooking the main street is the impressive, ancient Parish Church of St. Peter's which is usually left open for visitors. In the churchyard is a Norman chapel, with the familiar rounded doorway

arch. The river Bollin actually flows under the main street.

When in Prestbury look for Pearl Street and its weavers' cottages dated 1686.

Location: Prestbury is on the A538, two miles north of Macclesfield.

GAWSWORTH, near Macclesfield

For stunning beauty, Gawsworth's church, fish pools and Old Hall take some beating. Gawsworth Old Hall, seen across the water, is a dream in black and white timber. Dating from the fifteenth century, it has a tilting ground where, in medieval times, mounted knights would joust. The Old Hall, for which an admission charge is payable, is still a family home.

St James's Church contains monuments to the Fitton family, including the figure of Mary Fitton, said to have been the 'Dark Lady' of Shakespeare's sonnets. Opposite the church is the timber-framed Old Rectory. In a field used as a visitor car park, is a single-storey wooden building which serves as the local cafe.

Location: Gawsworth is off the A536, two miles south of Macclesfield.

The splendid doorway arch of the Norman chapel behind Prestbury Parish Church, near Macclesfield.
Elisabeth Rowlatt

THE MUSEUM OF SCIENCE AND INDUSTRY IN MANCHESTER

This outstanding Museum qualified for inclusion in this book only at the last minute.   On 1 April 2001 the £3.50 charge for the over sixties was scrapped, allowing them free admission.

And on 1 December, 2001 the £6.50 full adult admission charge was also scrapped. From this date all adults could get in free. The under eighteens already got in free. Admission charges to special temporary exhibitions continues.

The Museum located across Liverpool Road, from the Castlefield Canal Basin off Deansgate, occupies former railway warehouses. The warehouses were part of the original Manchester terminal of the Manchester to Liverpool railway that was open in 1830. Also part of the Museum is the world's first passenger railway station, Liverpool Road station. Here you can see the original booking office and hall, complete with waxwork figures of railway workers and passengers.

On the track outside, visitors enjoy short rides on replicas of the open topped railway carriages of 1830. The carriages are pulled by a replica of the locomotive Planet.

The Museum's other attractions include:

Air and Space Hall: Historic Flying Machines to Space Craft exhibits.

Underground Manchester: visit an reconstructed Victorian sewer. Discover Manchester's unhealthy sanitation in the nineteenth century.

Power Hall: Fabulous working displays of the steam engines and other machines invented during the Industrial Revolution.

Xperiment!: Fun for children in the hands-on science centre.

Electricity gallery: Includes a power station re-built here on site.

Gas gallery: Gas through the ages.

The Making of Manchester: The city's history.

Futures: A re-build of the world's first stored programme computer (assembled in Manchester).

A metrolink train runs through Piccadilly in Manchester city centre.

Location: Liverpool Road, off Deansgate.
Opening times: Every day from 10.00 am to 5.00 pm.
Telephone: 0161 832 2244.
Full disabled access available - except for one gallery.

MANCHESTER TOWN HALL

Report to Reception at Manchester Town Hall's Albert Square entrance, and they will give you a free pass which admits you to the first floor rooms.

A highlight is the Great Hall, the walls of which are covered with twelve mural paintings by Ford Madox Brown. They depict famous men and incidents in Manchester's proud history.

You also see the Mayor's Parlour, the Banquetting room with its Minstrels' Gallery, and other rooms. There is much fine furniture and beautiful stonework in the Town Hall's interior.

Opened in 1887, this truly magnificent Gothic building is crowned with an impressive clock tower 286 feet high.
Opening times: Monday to Friday 9.00 am to 5.00 pm. Closed Saturday except for guided tours (fee charged).
Telephone: 0161 234 5000.
Full disabled access available.

HEATON PARK

Everything about Heaton Park, on the outskirts of north Manchester, is on the grand scale. It is one of the largest local authority owned public park in Europe. Walk in the middle of its 648 acres of hilly open spaces and woods and you could be in the heart of rural Cheshire. Only by standing on one of the park's highest points can you see anything of the suburbs of Higher Blackley and Prestwich on opposite sides.

Apart from scenic charm, Heaton Park offers a wide range of recreational activities. It contains Heaton Hall, an important neo-classical mansion, which is open to the public, an excellent pets' corner and farm animals in the former estate's stables centre. There is also a very large, tree lined boating lake, which boasts two wooded islands.

On summer Sundays, single decked vintage trams give rides, starting from the park's Middleton Road entrance. There is also a free admission tramways museum here. The park also offers a range of sports, including an eighteen-hole public golf course.

Construction of the superb ten-acre boating lake began in 1908 as part of a Manchester City Council scheme to create employment. The lake occupies the site of a former racecourse, which operated on the Egerton family estate from 1825 to 1837.

Heaton Hall and its park were sold to Manchester City Council in 1902, by the Egerton family, owners of the estate since 1864, at which point John Egerton married heiress Elizabeth Holland. The Holland family had previously owned the estate since the Middle Ages. Sir Thomas Egerton, builder of the present mansion, was created first Earl of Wilton in 1801.

HEATON HALL

The house is open to the public from May to September, and at the time of writing admission was free. But the possibility of eventually charging for admission was being considered. However, a spokeswoman for Manchester City Council told me that they intended to carry out further restoration work on the house, before imposing a charge. There was also a plan to restore and open the hall's west wing.

National Lottery money is being sought to improve both the hall and park. Even in the event of admission charges, people should still be able to view the hall free from 4.00 pm onwards.

The interior of the hall is a magnificent sight, following a fifteen year refurbishment programme, involving, among other things, lashings of gold leaf. Of the rooms on view the circular dressing room of the Dowager Lady Egerton, is perhaps the most arresting. Eight mirrors are set between painted column-like sections of wall and

Roman triumphal arches, all trimmed with gold leaf. The ceiling is a splendid sight with its delicately painted panels. A chandelier completes the stunning effect. This room is a rare survivor of the popular 'Pompeian' style of the 1770s. There are only three such rooms in British houses open to the public.

Another re-decorated ceiling of great beauty, is to be found in the saloon. Heaton Hall's library, with its dark green walls and white ceiling, is another striking room. Here is to be found a picture of one of the many horse race meetings, held at Heaton Park. There are other rooms on show, notably the dining and music rooms. The latter has an eighteenth century organ filling up one wall.

Some of the original contents, previously belonging to the Egerton family, are still here, plus a great many pictures and much furniture imported from the City Council's art gallery collections.

Note: The Hall entrance is on the opposite side of the house to the gardens.

Opening times: May to September, Thursday to Sunday, 10.00 am to 5.30 pm. Sunday 2.00 pm to 5.30 pm. Visitors are advised to telephone before visiting to ensure that the Hall is open.

Full disabled access available.

Telephone: 0161 234 1456

CASTLEFIELD URBAN HERITAGE PARK, Manchester

Impressive railway viaducts, canals and a mock Roman fort gatehouse make this an historic city centre site worth walking round. It was here that the Romans built their fort in what is now Manchester. Here the Duke of Bridgewater's canal barges brought coal from his Worsley canal basin, which served his coal mines in that area.

At Castlefield one can walk a few yards from the Bridgewater Canal to the start of the Rochdale Canal. From Castlefield the world's first important passenger railway left the city for Liverpool. Old canal warehouses at Castlefield have been reconstructed for non-industrial use. There is an amphitheatre for outdoor events.

The fabulous Museum of Science and Industry at Manchester occupies what was the Liverpool Road railway station of 1830 and its carriage shed and warehouses.

Location: Castlefield is just off the south end of Deansgate.

DEBDALE PARK, Gorton

I have included this modest park because alongside and behind it are the Gorton Reservoirs, which feature creeks set in pleasant

surroundings. The walk through the park and round the reservoirs is one of about two and a half miles with no sign of the built-up suburbs of east Manchester. If you work up an appetite during this easy walk, there is a McDonald's restaurant outside the park!
Location: On A57 Manchester to Hyde Road.

GALLERY OF COSTUME, Platt Hall, Rusholme, Manchester

Platt Hall, a red brick Palladian mansion built in the mid 1700s, was bought with its estate by Manchester Corporation in 1908. Platt Fields was opened as a public park in 1910.

Clothes dating from the seventeenth century to modern times are displayed at Platt Hall, which stands at the north end of Platt Fields park at Wilmslow Road.

The City Council's spectacular dress collection is the largest of its type outside the Victoria and Albert Museum in London, but here at Platt Hall there is exhibition space for only a fraction, so exhibits are changed constantly. The Gallery of Costume is open from Tuesdays to Saturdays from 10.00 am throughout the year.

Eventually the collection may be moved to larger premises, so telephone 0161 224 5217 before visiting just in case!

Platt Fields park has a large boating lake and a lakeside cafe.
Location: The main entrance and Platt Hall are near the junction of Wilmslow Road and Platt Lane.
Full disabled access available.

MANCHESTER CRAFT CENTRE

Once Manchester's old fish and poultry market, this striking Victorian building, crowned with a huge glass roof, now provides a permanent working base for a diverse range of craftspeople and designers.

The centre, set in the maze of side streets north of Piccadilly Gardens, is one of the few places in the North West open to the public where goods are both produced and sold on the premises. Goods on show include jewellery, ceramics, sculpture, metalwork, fashion, furniture, textiles and glass. Exhibitions are held regularly. Visitors can get full meals in the cafe. There is a car park to the rear of the building.
Location: Oak Street (between Shudehill and Tib Street).
Opening times: Monday to Saturday, 10.00 am to 5.30 pm. (limited opening on Mondays). Open Sundays in December only.
Telephone: 0161 832 4274.
Partial disabled access only.

WYTHENSHAWE HALL AND PARK, Northenden

Thanks to the owners, Manchester City Council, Wythenshawe Hall is one old house you can view without paying an admission charge. There are six rooms on view and behind the hall, hidden inside high walls, are beautiful Victorian gardens. There is a excellent display of rhododendrons in May and June.

A few years ago the hall's black and white frontal decoration (put on in the 1940s) was removed and the timbers exposed to give the original sixteenth century look. Inside the hall the dining room is the building's most complete survival of the Tudor hall built by Robert Tatton. The Tatton family occupied Wythenshawe Hall from 1540 until 1926.

The house contains some fine pictures, and the drawing room features an unusual black and white frieze which celebrated the marriage that united the Tatton and Booth families in the fourteenth century. The frieze was discovered behind eighteenth century panelling.

In 1926 Robert Henry Greville Tatton sold the hall and estate to Ernest Simon (later Lord Simon of Wythenshawe). Simon, a former Lord Mayor of Manchester, immediately presented the hall and park to the city. Lord Simon was the visionary who planned the vast Wythenshawe council housing estate (hailed as Britain's garden city) which was built on the bulk of the country estate he had bought from the Tattons.

In front of the hall stands a statue of Oliver Cromwell, whose troops captured the hall in 1644.

Wythenshawe Hall, Manchester.

Statue of Oliver Cromwell at Wythenshawe Hall, Manchester.

Facilities: The 250 acres of Wythenshawe Park include a good pitch-and-putt course, and a marvellous Horticultural Centre. There are refreshments in the cafe at the horticultural centre.

Location: Park main entrance is on Wythenshawe Road, Northenden, near junction 9 of the M63.

Opening times: Wythenshawe Hall is open from late May to late September. Wednesday to Saturday 10.00 am to 12 noon and 1.00 pm to 5.30 pm. Sunday 2.00 pm to 5.30 pm. Closed Monday and Tuesday. Visitors are advised to ring 0161 998 2331 to check times. Full disabled access available.

WYTHENSHAWE PARK HORTICULTURAL CENTRE

This is well worth visiting, for there is a vast area under glass together with outside nurseries and landscaped grounds that include an impressive rockery and pond and herbaceous borders. Plants are on sale all year round.

Under glass, the Safari Walk leads the visitor past exotic plants like bananas, pineapples, rice and lemons, as well as carnivorous plants. The centre possesses a marvellous collection of cacti. In spring and summer the Bulb House presents a great display of flowers.

The latest attraction under glass is the Jungle Walk.

The Horticultural Centre has a basic cafe and shop.

Opening times: Open all year, seven days a week, from 10.00 am to 4.00 pm.

Telephone: 0161 945 1768.

Full disabled access available.

THE PUMPHOUSE PEOPLE'S HISTORY MUSEUM, Manchester

There is a small admission charge for this excellent new museum, opened in 1994. But every Friday is a free admission day for all. And pensioners, students and the unemployed are admitted free on any day, so the Pumphouse certainly qualifies for inclusion in this book!

Imaginative displays reconstruct the often grim lives of ordinary working people during the past 200 years, from Victorian cotton workers to today's footballers. The museum deals with the history of trades unions, and it possesses no less than 300 union banners. These colourful items are displayed on a rota basis on the walls.

The museum has been constructed inside the walls of a 1909 hydraulic pumping station, which served industry in the city centre until 1972. There is also a cafe.

Location: Bridge Street, off Deansgate.

Opening times: Tuesdays to Sundays, 11.00 am to 4.30 pm. Closed Mondays.

Telephone: 0161 839 6061.

Full disabled access available.

MANCHESTER CATHEDRAL, Victoria Street

Manchester Cathedral was founded as a collegiate church in 1421 but it was not given cathedral status until 1847 (it was greatly enlarged by the Victorians). So the 150th anniversary of Manchester Cathedral and the Diocese of Manchester was celebrated in 1997.

Although many churches are closed most of the time these days, to prevent vandalism and theft, Manchester Cathedral remains open seven days a week, thank goodness. The cathedral's outstanding feature is the beautifully carved choir stalls, executed by Tudor craftsmen. There are thirty canopied stalls, and underneath the choirstall seats are amusing carvings. They include a man fleeing from his wife after dropping a jug of ale; rabbits roasting a huntsman, and pigs dancing to bagpipes.

The cathedral is also noted for having the widest nave of any in the country, with the width of the building being two-thirds of its length.

It was originally a Saxon church, with a good deal of the existing structure dating from the fifteenth century. For information about the cathedral's brass rubbing centre ring the cathedral office on 0161 833 2220.

For details of free lunchtime recitals in the cathedral by pupils of the nearby Chetham's School of Music ring the school on 0161 834 9644.

In 2001 work began on providing a Visitor Centre at the Cathedral, on an adjacent site. Workmen uncovered medieval arches which will be incorporated into the Visitor Centre café in its basement. Diners will be able to see the arches as they eat.

Location: Near Victoria railway station.

Opening times: Times vary owing to the different services held in the Cathedral. Telephone to check before setting out.

Full disabled access available.

WHITWORTH ART GALLERY, Oxford Road, Manchester

Owned by Manchester University, this is one of Britain's leading provincial galleries and has a large collection in store. There is an important collection of British and foreign watercolours and

The Whitworth Art Gallery, Manchester.

drawings and the gallery is second only to the Victoria and Albert Museum in its range of textile exhibits from many parts of the world.

The red brick gallery was gifted to Manchester University in 1958 by the private trust which owned it and could not afford to continue doing so. It was built with money from the will of the famous Stockport-born machine tool manufacturer Sir Joseph Whitworth (1830-1887). He was the man who introduced uniformity into screw threads.

Location: On Oxford Road, near University, and almost opposite Manchester Royal Infirmary.

Opening times: Monday to Saturday 10.00 am to 5.00 pm. Sunday 2.00 pm to 5.00 pm.

Hot meals are available at the gallery bistro.

Telephone: 0161 275 7450.

Full disabled access available.

MANCHESTER MUSEUM, Manchester University, Oxford Road

Manchester Museum is so big that it is almost impossible to cover everything in one visit. Now, with a £12 million National Lottery grant, the museum has a five-year expansion plan that will add extra galleries, a restaurant and gift shop.

The museum's Egyptology collection, which features twenty-one mummies, is the best in Britain next to those in London and Oxford. Manchester Museum is unusual in possessing a wealth of material that illustrates everyday life in ancient Egypt, as well as from tombs.

The stunning new Mediterranean gallery will be of interest and children will enjoy the aquarium and vivarium. There is also an enormous collection of stuffed animals and birds, including a fully grown Bengal tiger, a lion and a polar bear.

Opening times: Monday to Saturday 10.00 am to 5.00 pm. Closed on Sundays.

Telephone: 0161 275 2634.

Full disabled access available.

THE JOHN RYLANDS LIBRARY, Deansgate, Manchester

This superb 1890s Gothic building could be seen as Manchester's Taj Mahal. The Taj Mahal at Agra was built by a man as a posthumous tribute to his wife. The John Rylands Library and its initial stock of rare books was financed by Enriqueta Augustina Rylands in memory of her husband John Rylands, the wealthy Manchester cotton merchant, after his death in 1888.

The stone building of great beauty took ten years to build and was

Two impressed visitors look at an exhibit in the Power Hall at the Museum of Science and Industry. Jean Horsfall

opened to the public on New Year's Day, 1900. It remained an independent library until 1972, when it merged with the Manchester University Library. The library houses the finest collection of rare books and manuscripts in the north of England.

Apart from viewing this fabulous building, visitors can see exhibitions which are always on view. At opposite ends of the reading room are statues in white marble of Mr and Mrs Rylands.

Opening times: Monday to Friday 10.00 am to 5.30 pm. Saturday 10.00 am to 1.00 pm.

Telephone: 0161 834 5343 or 6765.

Partial disabled access only.

GREATER MANCHESTER POLICE MUSEUM, Newton Street, Manchester

Set up in 1981, this museum occupies a former Victorian police station, built in 1879. It was an operational police station for ninety-nine years.

The building contains the original entrance hall complete with riot gates, the charge office and cell block on the ground floor, with various displays of police equipment. In the parade room and doctor's surgery on the upper floor are further displays of objects and photographs, which trace the history of the police service. In the former canteen there is a small display of international police uniforms and memorabilia.

Location: Halfway up Newton Street (which links Piccadilly with Great Ancoats Street).

Opening times: (at time of writing): Tuesdays only 10.00 am to 3.30 pm. Other weekdays by appointment only. Guided tours are available.

Telephone: 0161 856 3287.

Partial disabled access only.

FLETCHER MOSS BOTANICAL GARDENS, Wilmslow Road, Didsbury

Perhaps a dream of paradise might picture something like the spectacular rock garden here. The rock garden occupies a steep slope, with little winding paths among the beautiful flowering shrubs, heathers, cedars and other decorative trees. A rivulet pours down to a pond at the bottom. The rock garden, and lovely flower beds here, reflect great credit on Manchester City Council's gardeners. This is a much-loved spot; the many donated seats in memory of loved ones bear witness to that.

There are grass tennis courts for hire here and a cafe selling home-made cakes occupies one room of a private house that overlooks the rock garden. A plaque records that at a meeting in this room, the Royal Society for the Protection of Birds was founded in 1889.

Location: Main entrance to Botanical Gardens is in Stenner Lane (near *The Didsbury* and *Ye Old Cock* pubs and St. James's Church). Or alternatively, drive down Millgate Lane, off Wilmslow Road (A5145) to small car park near rock garden.

Next to the *Ye Old Cock* pub is the entrance to The Old Parsonage Gardens, also worth a visit. It has a rose garden and orchid house. From Stenner Lane there is a pleasant walk to the river Mersey.

MANCHESTER CITY ART GALLERIES

The big municipal art galleries in Manchester and Liverpool are considered to have the best collections outside London. And as I write this, the Manchester galleries in Mosley Street and adjoining Princess Street are being linked up by the construction of a large extension. This exciting project will mean that eventually a great deal more of the permanent collection will be on view at any one time. However, the building work has resulted in both galleries being closed for three years from 1998. The scheduled re-opening date was the spring of 2002.

The main gallery in Mosley Street was established in 1882 after

Manchester corporation took over the building and collections of the Royal Manchester Institution. The Grade One listed building – completed in 1834 in Greek Revival style – was designed by Sir Charles Barry, architect of the Houses of Parliament. The collection is best known internationally for its Pre-Raphaelites, including twenty-nine oil paintings by Ford Madox Brown. Competing for importance are the eighteenth and early nineteenth century British schools that preceded the Pre-Raphaelites and the high Victorian, Edwardian and British modern schools that followed. And Dutch and Flemish seventeenth and eighteenth century paintings form a group of ninety that are unequalled outside London. It is a stunning show of traditional art, sculpture and ceramics in a fabulous building that, happily, is open on Sundays.

The Princess Street gallery round the corner, formerly a gentleman's club, was also designed by Sir Charles Barry and has been used to display temporary exhibitions. Also in Princess Street is the entrance to an excellent cafe, recommended in *The Good Food Guide*.

Opening times: Monday 11.00 am to 5.30 pm. Tuesday to Saturday 10.00 am to 5.30 pm. Sunday 2.00 pm to 5.30 pm.

Telephone: 0161 234 1456.

Full disabled access available.

PORTICO LIBRARY AND GALLERY

Near the City Art Gallery, at the junction of Moseley Street and Charlotte Street, is the Portico Library and Gallery. Opened in 1806, the Portico is a private library. But regular art exhibitions are held here which are open to the public. The entrance is the first door in Charlotte Street.

Opening times: Monday to Friday, 9.30 am to 4.30 pm.

Telephone: 0161 236 6785.

No specific access for the disabled.

CHETHAM'S LIBRARY TOUR AND FREE MUSIC RECITAL

Fascinating medieval buildings surround a huge courtyard on the Chetham's School of Music site, which is located between Manchester Cathedral and the city's Victoria railway station.

There are free tours of Chetham's Library of ancient books, plus certain other parts of the fifteenth century buildings. The short tours take place on Wednesday afternoons during term times at the School of Music. It starts with a recital by School of Music pupils in the Baronial Hall at 1.35 pm, followed by refreshments. After this the tour takes in the Baronial Hall, followed by the cloisters section and then the Reading Room of the library. Here you can see ancient books that were chained up to prevent theft. Chetham's library was

founded in 1653 and is the oldest in the English speaking world. It is housed in a building that dates from 1421.
Location: Long Millgate, Manchester.
Telephone: 0161 834 7961.
Full disabled access available.

PANKHURST CENTRE, Chorlton-on-Medlock, Manchester

Emmeline Pankhurst, the famous campaigner for votes for women, lived at 62 Nelson Street, with her daughters and fellow suffragettes, Christabel and Sylvia, from 1897 to 1907. She founded the Women's Social and Political Union at a meeting at the house in 1903. Number 62 and the adjoining house, which are located beside Manchester Royal Infirmary, have been restored and turned into a marvellous centre for women. The story of women's suffrage is told here, and there is also the Pankhurst Parlour, furnished in Edwardian style.

The Pankhurst Centre is open from Monday to Friday only, from 10.00 am to 3.00 pm. Cafe and gift shop.
Location: Nelson Street, off Oxford Street.
Telephone: 0161 273 5673.
Note: The Whitworth Art Gallery and Manchester Museum are nearby for those who want a full afternoon out.
Partial disabled access only.

CONTEMPORARY FINE ART GALLERIES

These galleries are at Manchester Metropolitan University (Faculty of Art and Design). There are three art galleries – the John Holden and the Righton Gallery which are in Grosvenor Building, Cavendish Street, All Saints (off Oxford Road) and the Aytoun Street Gallery (paintings and photography) in Aytoun Street, just off Piccadilly.

The galleries are in university buildings, so to get directions and to find out what is on, ring 0161 247 1708. Galleries open Monday to Friday 10.00 am to 5.00 pm. There are no exhibitions during university holidays in July and August.
Full disabled access available.

CORNERHOUSE

Centre for international cinema. Three galleries have changing exhibitions of photography, sculpture and paintings. There is a bar and a cafe. Galleries are open Tuesday to Saturday, 11.00 am to 6.00 pm.
Location: 70 Oxford Road, Manchester.
Telephone: 0161 236 7323.
Full disabled access available.

Northwich and Winsford

BLAKEMERE CRAFT CENTRE, Sandiway, near Northwich

Most of the craft shops are in a restored Edwardian stable block built around a courtyard. Blakemere Hall was demolished in 1950 and the masonry and internal panelling shipped to America. More recently the stable block was used to house race horses and a piggery.

An interesting feature for visitors is the birds of prey centre. There is also an aquatic centre, an indoor children's play centre, a pottery and blacksmith, plus a restaurant.

In the 1890s Edward VII, then Prince of Wales, visited Blakemere regularly and notorious wild parties are said to have taken place, after which joiners were employed to repair the furniture.

Location: On A556 near its junction with the A49, midway between Northwich and Chester.

Opening times: Tuesday to Friday 10.00 am to 5.00 pm. Saturdays and Sundays 10.00 am to 5.30 pm. (closed Mondays).

Telephone: 01606 883261.

Full disabled access available except for three units. No disabled access to special Craft Fairs.

LITTLE BUDWORTH COUNTRY PARK

Follow the Heathland Trail at Little Budworth Country Park and explore its ancient heathland and mires which are rare habitats, home to grass snakes, lizards and other unusual plants and animals. This small country park also features birch and oak woodland.

Nearby Little Budworth village is worth visiting. This is a good locality for charming villages like Tarporley, Utkinton, Kelsall, Tarvin and Eaton.

Location: Little Budworth is one mile east of the A49 Warrington to Whitchurch Road and next to Oulton Park motor racing circuit.

DELAMERE FOREST

One does not have to own a car to get to Delamere Forest for Delamere railway station, on the Manchester to Chester line, is at the southern tip of the forest. And not far away is the Linmere Visitor centre. In the car park here the Groundwork Trust runs a cycle hire facility at weekends and Bank Holidays from April to September and daily during school summer holidays.

Cyclists can explore the area on marked routes of four miles or seven miles. For walkers, the main users of Delamere Forest, there are also marked trails. Thanks to the route signs, and maps available at the Visitor centre, it is very difficult to get lost! And there are cafes at Delamere railway station and at Hatch Mere, the largest of the forest's many areas of water.

Delamere Forest is partly on undulating land, so walkers enjoy more open views than are to be had in many other wooded areas. Delamere includes our largest forest nursery, producing half the trees needed annually by the Forestry Commission. Today the main conifer species in the adult woods is Corsican pine, with Scots pine, larch, and western hemlock also present. Broad-leaved species such as oak, ash, beech, birch, sycamore and rowan are used to add variety to the landscape.

Location: Delamere Forest is a mile north of the A556 road from Northwich, where it joins the A54. There is also a Visitor Centre.
Telephone: 01606 882167.

MARBURY COUNTRY PARK, near Northwich

A walk beside Budworth Mere, one of Cheshire's loveliest lakes, is the feature of Marbury Country Park. It is an idyllic scene when dozens of yachts are sailing. Rhododendrons and attractive trees border the lakeside path. Marbury Hall, a nineteenth century mansion, once stood here.

The country park's entrance is on the Comberbach to Barnton road, two miles north of the centre of Northwich. Two other tourist attractions are not far away. At Anderton is the famous Anderton Lift, which has being renovated; a massive device that hoists boats from the River Weaver Navigation to the Trent and Mersey Canal.

And near Budworth Mere stands the Tudor village of Great Budworth, one of the most beautiful villages in the North West. The gem of a parish church here has a wonderful interior full of quaint carvings. The village's brick and timber cottages and thatched roofs complete a perfect setting.

WINSFORD FLASH

Winsford in central Cheshire is a town of two halves, for it straddles the steep-sided valley of the river Weaver. On the south side of town is the Bottom Flash, a lake which stretches for nearly a mile in a setting of great beauty. Bottom Flash was created after the valley floor subsided around 1850 due to collapsed underground salt workings. It retained overflow water from the river which flows into the lake from the east side.

From the massive roundabout which straddles the river in the open, 'middle' of Winsford there is a marked footpath beside the river as it leaves the Bottom Flash. After crossing meadowland beside the flash the right of way is along a lane high above the lake which gives fabulous views across the valley.

The walker passes two upmarket caravan sites which are worth visiting. The sites – with moorings for boats – are on steeply sloping ground above the lake, in a picturesque setting. Many of the caravans have lovely gardens. The activities of the Winsford Flash Sailing Club adds to the interest.

From the lane near the caravan sites a path leads westwards to the lovely St Chad's Church where a cafe is open on Saturdays in summer. If you wish to drive to the lake and caravan sites you can do so from the west side of town (Way's Green area).

Oldham

OLDHAM'S NEW ART GALLERY

The Oldham Art Gallery in Union Street closed in January, 2001, for over a year. But local art lovers were excited about this for a new three storey Art Gallery has been built behind it and was opened in February of 2002.

The new Art Gallery is a long, slim edifice with many large windows, and with balconies on the third floor on which visitors can stand and gaze at the hills around the town. There is also a cafe and gift shop. This building, together with a large new library and performing arts facility on the site, will eventually comprise the grandly named 'Oldham Cultural Quarter'.

Crane your necks to see this - Oldham's new Art Gallery under construction.
Elisabeth Rowlatt

Oldham's war memorial, with the parish church.

Meanwhile the Union Street building, which comprises the old library on the ground floor and the old Art Gallery on the first floor, remains in use. Oldham Museum in nearby Greaves Street, closed in June, 2000. Its exhibits were being moved into the Union Street building.

The old purpose built Library and Art Gallery in Union Street was presented to the town by local mill owner and philanthropist Charles Lees.

The new Art Gallery is connected to the Union Street building by a footbridge linking up what are now two art galleries. There is more space at last to hang the town's permanent collection.

Since Oldham is built on the side of a moor, you will need a warm coat on a cold winter's day! The town still has a Lowry-like appearance with huge mills towering over terraced streets. (It once boasted 320 mills). Since the decline of the textile industry most mills are now used for other trades and businesses.

Location: In town centre off Union Street.

Opening times: Not available at time of writing.

Telephone: 0161 911 4657

Full disabled access available.

UPPERMILL, near OLDHAM

This old textile manufacturing village is in the Tame Valley a few miles east of Oldham. It becomes a favourite day out for tourists on Sundays, for the one main street contains gift shops and cafes, plus Saddleworth Museum and Art Gallery (admission charge).

The Huddersfield Narrow Canal, which runs near the main street, has been restored. Early in 2001 the three-miles long Standedge Tunnel which takes the canal under the Pennines at Diggle was re-opened to pleasure boats. The canal emerges in Yorkshire at Marsden. It is a lovely three mile walk from Uppermill, along the canal, to Diggle. Return by bus from Diggle if required.

TANDLE HILL COUNTRY PARK, ROYTON

This small country park features a deep glen and a fine view across to Rochdale and Bury from the top of Tandle Hill. The park was a gift to the public, just after the Great War, as a thanks offering for peace by a local landowner.

Location: Just off the A671 Oldham to Rochdale road, two miles north of Oldham town centre.

DAISY NOOK COUNTRY PARK, near Failsworth.

Daisy Nook. The name conjures up a sunlit corner out of the wind. Certainly this part of the valley of the river Medlock, northeast of Manchester, is a surprisingly pleasant green oasis wedged between Oldham and Ashton-under-Lyne.

The new section of the M60, built across the Medlock Valley near Daisy Nook, does not affect the country park, which is centred on an old canal system built to serve cotton mills and collieries. Crime Lake, which features a variety of wildfowl, is at the end of an isolated canal section and was formed as a result of the canal construction in 1794.

From Crime Lake you can enjoy a circular walk along the Medlock Valley. Follow the canal to the Oldham to Ashton Road (A627) and walk back along a path high above the river Medlock where the National Trust owns land. You can cross the Medlock on an aqueduct. There is a visitor centre at Daisy Nook which offers refreshments.

Further up the valley, the other side of the A627, Park Bridge stands in a remote spot. It is an old ironworks village created by the Lees family in the 1850s. Stables here have been converted into an excellent heritage centre which is worth visiting.

Location: Daisy Nook is on the Ashton to Failsworth road. You can also walk into the country park from the car park just off the A627.

TOMMYFIELD MARKET, Oldham

This is believed to be the largest open air market in England. Tommyfield has about 300 traders. It is also claimed to be the highest permanent open air market in the country and although it is in the town centre it is at moorland height.

Opening times: Monday, Friday, Saturday, with a Flea Market on Wednesday. Open 9.00 am to 5.00 pm.

The big adjacent market hall is open Monday to Saturday 9.00 am to 5.00 pm.

The Peak District

CASTLETON, Derbyshire

If asked to name the most interesting village in the Peak District, many people would plump for Castleton. This tourist mecca in the High Peak offers great views of the so-called Shivering Mountain, Mam Tor and the high ridge to Lose Hill, with the spectacular Winnats Pass just up the road.

The nearby Blue John and Treak Cliff caverns are believed to be the world's only source of the semi-precious Blue John fluorspar which is made into beautiful vases and all sorts of trinkets for the tourists and sold in Castleton's shops. In one shop there is a small

A view of Peakshole Water in Castleton village, looking towards the entrance to the famous Peak Cavern. Kath Hodgson

Blue John museum containing a table with a circular top made entirely of the purple-blue stone and put together in sections.

Castleton's visitors, including hordes of hungry hikers, have the choice of several excellent cafes in this lively place. Its attractions include the ruins of Peveril Castle on its crag above the village and the spectacular Peak Cavern (admission charges to both places). Below Peveril Castle is the almost hidden entrance to secluded Cave Dale, which runs up onto the moors south of the village.

The A625 Sheffield to Chapel-en-le-Frith road passes through Castleton, only to end abruptly well short of the Winnats Pass with a 1½ mile gap before it resumes far above! It has been like this since 1976 when a landslip from the treacherous shale and gritstone face of Mam Tor caused the road below to collapse and never to be opened again. So, the one-in-five minor road up the Winnats Pass is now the only link between the Manchester and Sheffield sides of the High Peak hereabouts. Landslips from Mam Tor regularly damaged the A625 before it was finally abandoned.

In this area are the Blue John, Speedwell and Treak Cliff caverns (admission charges).

PEAK DISTRICT WELL DRESSINGS

A visit to some of the delightful villages and towns in Derbyshire should include the amazing well dressings tableaux that are created throughout the county. Pagan water worship was forbidden by the early Christians but Tissington village revived the ancient well dressing custom in 1349.

The stunning pictures in flower petals and mosses, pressed onto a base of clay, stand several feet high. They are mounted on wooden frames and villagers work for several days on the project. Because the tableaux are exhibited for a week, a car run around Derbyshire allows you to see two or three in a day. At Tissington, near Ashbourne, six wells are dressed but most villages dress just one or two. The floral works of art usually have a religious theme.

There are sixty-seven places which dress wells. A list of festival dates for each year, plus times of the well blessing services, is available by telephoning the Buxton Tourist Information Centre on 01298 25106.

The following is a short list of the well dressings within a reasonable drive of Greater Manchester, leaving out villages in the Derby, Chesterfield and Matlock areas.

May: Tissington, Endon (near Leek), Middleton-by-Youlgreave, Youlgreave, Monyash.

June: Cressbrook (Millers Dale), Ashford-in-the-Water,

Chelmorton, Tideswell, Litton, Rowsley, Hope, Bakewell.
July: Hathersage, Chapel-en-le-Frith, Baslow, Buxton, Bamford, Peak Forest, Great Longstone, Little Longstone, Stoney Middleton.
August: Bradwell, Great Hucklow, Taddington, Eyam, Foolow, Wormhill.
September: Longnor, Hartington.

PAVILION GARDENS, Buxton
Located in the centre of Buxton, the Pavilion Gardens were laid out in 1871 as a Victorian park, with landscaped gardens and lakes. Since then some features have been lost, but the gardens, always delightful, are being restored to their Victorian magnificence with a £3.3 million Lottery grant. The improvements will be completed in 2002. The free admission gardens feature a miniature railway. The pavilion itself is an impressive building containing a cafe. A wide range of events is held there, from antique and craft fairs to dancing and concerts.
Opening times: Summer 10.00 am to 5.30 pm. Winter 10.00 am to 3.30 pm. Open seven days a week throughout the year.
Telephone: 01298 23114.

BUXTON MUSEUM AND ART GALLERY
Free admission to ground floor only (small admission charge for Wonders of the Peak Exhibition and upper floor art gallery). The building boasts three art galleries.
Opening times: Tuesday to Friday 9.30 am to 5.30 pm. Saturday 9.30 am to 5.00 pm. Sunday (Easter to September only) 10.30 am to 5.30 pm.
Location: Terrace Road, near Pavilion Gardens.
Telephone: 01298 24658.
Partial disabled access only.

MANOR PARK AND OLD GLOSSOP
Manor Park, on the eastern side of Glossop town centre, is a beautiful place that features a boating lake and miniature train rides. If you visit this excellent park have a look at adjoining Old Glossop, an enclave of seventeenth and eighteenth century cottages. There are cobbled pavements and an old village square and market place, as Old Glossop was the town's original centre.

Glossop lies below the high moors of northwest Derbyshire, so is a dramatic place to visit. The town has an indoor market on Thursday, Friday and Saturday and an outdoor market on Friday and Saturday.

The new Millennium Walkway in the Torrs Gorge, at New Mills. Kath Hodgson

Children play at the river Sett outside Hayfield parish church in Derbyshire. Kath Hodgson

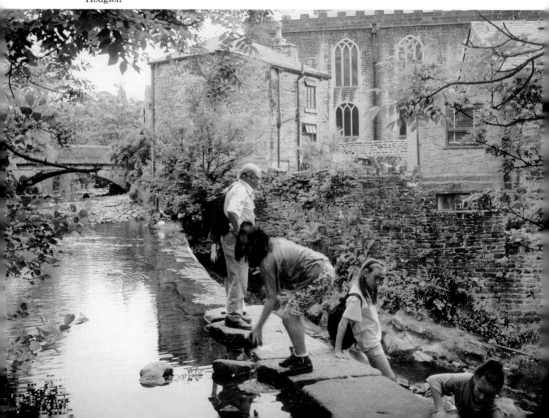

MILLENNIUM WALKWAY, New Mills

The spectacular river Goyt gorge at New Mills has an equally impressive addition. This is the 175-yard-long Torrs Millennium Walkway, built above the river at a cost of some £860,000. The year 2000 saw tourists walking along this part of the gorge for the first time thanks to the extraordinary bridge. The river Sett joins the Goyt at The Torrs. There are views of weirs, stone viaducts and awesome cliffs.

NEW MILLS HERITAGE AND INFORMATION CENTRE

A simulated coal mine and a wonderful model of the town as it was in 1884 are two features of New Mills Heritage Centre. The centre is housed in a refurbished stone building of character next to the bus station and near the railway station. It contains displays on the history of New Mills, a video and changing temporary exhibitions.
Location: Rock Mill Lane.
Opening times: Tuesday to Friday 11.00 am to 4.00 pm. Saturday and Sunday 10.30 am to 4.30 pm. (4.00 pm. in winter) Open Bank Holiday Mondays.
Telephone: 01663 746904.
Full disabled access available.
Note: For easy walking and wonderful views take the Sett Valley Trail from New Mills to Hayfield along the former railway line. Return by bus if desired.

BUXTON COUNTRY PARK

This country park occupies a stamina-sapping hill which rises to more than 1,400 feet above sea level and 400 feet above Buxton town. At the top is Solomon's Temple, a Victorian folly built in 1896. Visitors can climb a spiral staircase to the top of the tower for great views of Buxton and the surrounding hills.

The country park's entrance is at the car park of the famous Poole's Cavern which is open from March to October (admission charge). From here, there is a trail through Grinlow Woods to the summit. These woods were planted in 1800 to hide the scars of limestone quarrying. Buxton Country Park is a designated site of special scientific interest, partly because of the orchids that grow here.
Location: Green Lane, Buxton.
Telephone: 01298 26978.

Preston and Chorley

ASTLEY HALL, Chorley

Astley Hall is included in this book because admission is free to everyone living in the Borough of Chorley, provided they produce proof of their address. For the rest of us it is £2.95 for adults and £1.95 for concessions. However, I have arranged with the curator for two visitors to be admitted for the price of one if you show this book on entry to the Hall.

The hall, set in a beautiful wooded park of generous proportions, was donated to the people of Chorley in 1922, since when it has been the town's museum. The building was extensively reconstructed in the seventeenth century but much Elizabethan work survives including the courtyard. The south front has a 'wall of glass' appearance.

Outside the hall there is a lovely lily-covered lake and Astley Park features a spacious pets' corner. There is a cafe near the hall.

Location: One mile west of Chorley town centre, off A581, Southport Road.

Opening times: April to October: Tuesday to Sunday, noon to 5.00 pm. November to March: Friday to Sunday, noon to 4.00 pm.

Telephone: 01257 515555.

Partial disabled access only. Disabled admitted free to ground floor rooms.

PRESTON DOCK

At one time Preston was a thriving port for small cargo ships. Now the land around the enormous dock, which is half a mile long and several hundred yards wide, has been developed as a shopping and residential area. The dock, with access to the nearby river Ribble, is now a pleasure boat marina at the sea end, which gives interest to the walk around the dock side.

One side of Preston Dock is occupied by large stores, the other by flats. There is a restaurant in Morrison's supermarket and two pubs also serving meals.

Location: Preston Dock is at Riversway, west of Preston town centre.

THE ANTIQUE CENTRE, Preston

The former Preston Methodist Church and school in Garstang Road is now an excellent antiques centre, with around thirty dealers offering a wide range of goods. Many of the units are in the old gallery where there is a cafe. Go straight through the back of the old church into the adjoining school building, where there are many shops.

Location: North of town centre on the A6 Garstang Road.
Opening times: Open seven days a week.
Telephone: 01772 882078.
Partial disabled access only.

HARRIS MUSEUM AND ART GALLERY, Preston

This magnificent building is like a piece of Athens in Preston. The Harris was built on a monumental scale and is regarded as one of the best examples of late Greek Revival architecture in Britain.

In 1877 local lawyer, Edmund Robert Harris, left the then colossal sum of £300,000 to Preston in memory of his father, the Reverend Robert Harris, who had been Vicar of St George's church for sixty-

The Harris Museum and Art Gallery. Harris Museum

four years. One third of the money was allocated to the building and furnishing of the Free Library, Museum and Art Gallery. The laying of the foundation stone for the Harris building formed part of the Preston Guild celebrations in 1882.

The building – inside and out – is graced with impressive sculptured figures, classical friezes and murals. They include the Greek figures on the pediment above the outside columns, the Parthenon sculptures on the first and second floor balconies, the frieze room from the Temple of Apollo Epicurios, the Triumph of Alexander frieze and the Egyptian murals seventy feet above the central hall. (Tours of the balcony can be arranged to view these).

Despite the size of the museum and art gallery, only a small proportion of the vast collections can be exhibited at one time, along with touring exhibitions. British paintings from the seventeenth century onwards form a large part of the art collection. But the main aim is to present key examples of contemporary British art. There is a large number of late nineteenth century and early twentieth century sculptures.

There are galleries devoted to ceramics, glass, costume, local and social history and archaeology. Visitors can learn about the famous Preston Guild celebrations which have taken place every twenty years since 1542, about the decisive civil war Battle of Preston in 1648 and the 150 years' domination of Preston by the cotton industry.

Location: The Harris is in the town centre, at Market Square.
Opening times: Monday to Saturday 10.00 am to 5.00 pm. Closed Sundays.
Cafe open to 4.00 pm.
Telephone: 01772 258248.
Full disabled access available.

BEACON FELL COUNTRY PARK, near Longridge

Eight miles north of Preston, Beacon Fell Country Park comprises an area of coniferous, deciduous and mixed woodland with some rough moorland. Beacon Fell (873 feet) is an isolated hill on the edge of the Bowland Fells. From the summit visitors are rewarded with superb views. There is a pretty tarn, with an island, on the lower slopes.

Walking guides are available from the Visitor centre – there are also colour-coded waymarked walks of half a mile, one and a half miles and two and a half miles. Records show that there was a beacon at the summit as long ago as 1002 A.D. Beacon Fell was

designated as a country park in 1969, becoming one of the first in England.
Location: East of the M6 between junctions 32 (south) and 33 (north).
Telephone: 01995 561693.

THE OLD GRAMMAR SCHOOL, LEYLAND

The Old Grammar School, dating from 1524, was restored by South Ribble Borough Council in 1977 and opened as a local museum and arts centre. Two-thirds of the surviving building dates from 1580, so this museum is most interesting. The Leyland Free Grammar School finally closed in 1876 after a life of around 300 years.

The former ground floor schoolroom, with its original beams, houses an exhibition centre with monthly shows, many by local artists. The upper floor, an interesting series of small rooms, houses the borough's museum collection. The walls are of sixteenth century staff and daub with black and white timber frame construction.

Exhibits include an illuminated address commemorating the life and achievements of the great contralto, Kathleen Ferrier, who was born at Higher Walton, near Preston. The document was drawn up by the old Walton-le-Dale Urban District Council after the singer's death. Kathleen Ferrier's father was a teacher.
Location: The Old Grammar School is in Church Road in the centre of town, and next to the Parish Church.
Opening times: Thursday, 1.00 pm to 4.00 pm. Saturday, 10.00 am to 1.00 pm.
Telephone: 01772 422041.
No specific disabled access.

CUERDEN VALLEY COUNTRY PARK, Leyland

Cuerden Valley Country Park, just east of the town of Leyland, occupies more than 650 acres of pleasant countryside alongside the river Lostock. There is a fishing lake and woodlands.
Location: Entrance and car park is on Clayton Green Road, the B5256 to Leyland. Turn off A6 at Whittle-le-Woods. Leave M6 at junction 28 or the M61 at Junctions 8 or 9.

PRESTON MARKET, Earl Street

Opening times: The Market Hall is open Monday to Saturday. Outdoor market Monday, Wednesday, Friday and Saturday. Car boot market Tuesday and Thursday.
Telephone: 01772 906048.

CEDAR FARM GALLERIES, Mawdesley

Cedar Farm Galleries is set in the pretty village of Mawdesley which lies deep in an area of rural lanes. It is about six miles west of Chorley and two miles north of Parbold. The craft centre occupies stone-built barns on a pig farm. There is a crafts gallery and clothes and food shops. In a separate barn artists and craftspeople are working. The tea room serves full meals. Visitors can also see an area occupied by animals.

Location: Gorsey Lane, Mawdesley. The village is near the B5246 Rufford to Parbold road.

Opening times: Tuesday to Sunday 10.00 am to 5.00 pm.

Telephone: 01704 822038.

Partial disabled access only.

GUY'S THATCHED HAMLET, near Preston

This is a hotel and restaurant complex alongside the Lancaster canal. Craft and gift shops, ice cream parlour, childrens' play area, cricket ground and crown green bowls. Leaflets available describing a four mile walk from here, along the canal and the river Brock.

Location: St Michael's Road, Bilsborrow, Preston.

Telephone: 01995 640010.

Full disabled access available.

Rochdale

ESPLANADE ARTS AND HERITAGE CENTRE, Rochdale

This attractive stone faced building adorns The Esplanade, the wide street built over the river Roch in the centre of town.

At the time of writing (January 2002), Rochdale's Art Gallery and local studies centre here was still closed because of re-construction of the building's interior. The building was scheduled to re-open in May 2002, but this date saw only the Art Gallery open to the public.

The new museum which is being created here is due to open in the autumn of 2002. At the same time the facilities will be vastly improved with the addition of a Life Arts Theatre, a local studies centre, a book shop, a tourist information centre and a café. This will then be a splendid attraction.

Opening times: Not decided at time of writing.
Telephone: 01706 342154 for further details.
Full disabled access available.

ROCHDALE TOWN HALL

Also on The Esplanade is Rochdale Town Hall, a real piece of civic pride in stone, with its clock tower looking like Big Ben. The beautiful interior is worth seeing if you can persuade someone to show you round. The fabulous Great Hall has a hammerbeam roof and stained glass windows depicting the kings and queens of England.

Behind and above the Town Hall, on higher ground, is Rochdale Parish Church. This is open from May to September from 2.00 pm to 4.00 pm, Monday to Friday.
Full disabled access available.

HOLLINGWORTH LAKE AND COUNTRY PARK, near Rochdale

For more than 100 years Hollingworth Lake, with its amusement arcades, cafes and pubs, has been a celebrated spot for trippers. Now a country park has been created on the south side of the lake, with a wildfowl reserve. At the north end of the lake is an impressive purpose-built visitor centre with a cafe, exhibition hall and a plush lecture theatre in which you can see a film about the area.

On Lake Bank, or the lake front, you can hire rowing and motor boats and there are motor launch trips round the lake from April through to September. There is a lovely walk of just over two miles

Figures in stone on the front of Rochdale Art Gallery.

round the lake.

In the old days, Hollingworth Lake was known as The Weavers' Seaport because it was the nearest to the seaside that many of them could afford to get to. In the 1890s there was a funfair and the lake must then have had a strong seaside flavour.

The lake was created by flooding the fields from moorland streams. Three embankments were built to hold the water and the vast lodge, completed in 1804, was used to supply compensation water to the newly opened Rochdale Canal. The lake still supplies water to the long closed canal, the water being used by factories alongside it.

Hollingworth Lake owes much of its beauty to the hills which partly surround it. Rakewood Viaduct, which carries the M62 over a ravine-like valley here, is a dramatic sight with a height of 140 feet.

Location: The lake is on the Milnrow to Littleborough road (B6225).

Rochdale Town Hall. Elisabeth Rowlatt

The Great Hall at Rochdale Town Hall. Rochdale Borough Council

The Mayor's parlour at Rochdale Town Hall. Rochdale Borough Council

THE SHIPPON, Lower Ogden, Newhey, near Rochdale
The Shippon is a conversion of a farm building to an arts, crafts and gifts centre with a tea shop in a separate barn. It is situated amid grand moorland scenery near the Ogden Reservoir half a mile east of Newhey. There is a country park walk around three reservoirs. Newhey is at junction 21 of the M62.
Opening times: Every Sunday and Bank Holiday 1.00 pm to 6.00 pm. Also Saturdays from September to Christmas, 2.00 pm to 6.00 pm.
Telephone: 01706 847958.

ALL IN ONE GARDEN CENTRE, Middleton
This garden centre possesses both extensive showrooms and a large outdoor display area. A small pet and aquatic section. Pleasant and roomy restaurant with outdoor dining patio.
Opening times: Monday to Friday 8.30 am to 7.45 pm. Saturday 8.30 am to 6.00 pm. Sunday, 10.00 am to 4.30 pm.
Location: Rochdale Road, Middleton.
Telephone: 01706 711711.
Full disabled access available.

THE OLD GRAMMER SCHOOL, Middleton
This Elizabethan school of 1586 has been beautifully restored with a Lottery Grant.
Opening times: Tuesday to Saturday, 1.30 pm to 4.00 pm.
Location: Boarshaw Road, Middleton.

LITTLEBOROUGH COACH HOUSE, Littleborough
This local heritage and information centre is a shop window for local artists and craftspeople.
   Situated in the town centre behind *The Falcon* pub, the Coach House was built around 1800 as a staging post for the nearby turnpike. From Littleborough there is a marvellous walk to Todmorden along the Rochdale Canal, with moorland on both sides. The return journey can be made by bus or train.
Opening times: Tuesday, Wednesday, Thursday and Friday, 1.30 pm to 4.00 pm. Saturday, 11.00 am to 4.00 pm. Closed on Mondays.
Light refreshments available.
Telephone: 01706 378481.
Full disabled access available.

GREATER MANCHESTER FIRE SERVICE MUSEUM, Maclure Road, Rochdale

Opening times: Open to the public by appointment only.
Telephone: 01706 341221 for mutually convenient date and time.

WHITWORTH MUSEUM, Whitworth, near Rochdale

Run by the people of this small town north of Rochdale, Whitworth Museum has restricted opening times at the time of writing. It contains photographs, clothing, jewellery, militaria and old household appliances.
Location: North Street.
Opening times: Saturday 2.00 pm to 4.00 pm. Tuesday: 7.30 pm to 9.00 pm.
Telephone: 01706-343231.
Full disabled access available.

WARDLE, near Rochdale

Two lanes lead from the Rochdale to Littleborough road into Wardle village. And that's where they end, for this stone built village is up a cul-de-sac in the hills, amid splendid surroundings.

Wardle's large village square is impressive with its two large stone-faced chapels standing rather grandly side by side. A short uphill walk from the village brings the visitor to Watergrove Reservoir, which when built submerged a village of that name. The moors here are rich in footpaths.

HEALEY DELL NATURE TRAIL, near Whitworth

Healey Dell is a ravine that is in the centre of a nature reserve. The river Spodden rushes over rocks and under a 100 foot high viaduct that once carried the Rochdale to Bacup branch railway line (closed 1967).

The three mile nature trail is a most interesting walk. At one stage it crosses the top of the viaduct but much of the trail, being at the bottom of a ravine, is a good place to walk away from biting east winds in winter. The dell entrance road is at the junction of the A671 from Rochdale to Whitworth, and the B6377 (Shawclough Road). You might be able to get a trail guide from the newsagent's shop near the entrance.
Location: Healey Dell is 2½ miles north of Rochdale town centre. The trail starts at the warden's office.
Telephone: 01706 350459.

THE CORGI HERITAGE CENTRE, 53, York Street, Heywood
Do you remember the Corgi die-cast model vehicles you played with as a child? This museum and shop traces the history of the Corgi company from its early days as Mettoy, before the Second World War, to the present day. Vintage Corgi models galore are on show.
Location: Five minutes from Junctions 19 and 20 of the M62. Situated on the A58 in Heywood, between Rochdale and Bury.
Opening times: From 9.00 am to 5.30 pm on Monday, Wednesday, Thursday, Friday and Saturday.
Telephone: 01706 365812.

GORDON RIGGS GARDEN CENTRE, Walsden
Established more than fifty years ago, this big garden centre covers five acres, with two acres under cover. Late hours opening.
Note: No cafe or restaurant.
Mill shop cafe over the road.
Location: On main Rochdale to Todmorden Road.
Opening times: Monday to Friday 9.00 am to 9.00 pm. Saturday 9.00 am to 5.30 pm. Sunday 11.00 am to 5.00 pm.
Telephone: 01706 813374.
Full disabled access available.

TODMORDEN STEAM CENTRE TRUST, Todmorden Railway Station
Exhibits about the history of the local railway are on display. It opens at weekends from 1st May to late September. Admission is free but donations are welcome. Telephone first if making a special journey on 01706 816580. Strictly speaking Todmorden is in the West Yorkshire district of Calderdale but historically the county boundary splits the town and the town hall has a sign showing cotton to the west (Lancashire) and wool to the east (Yorkshire).

Rossendale Valley

ROSSENDALE MUSEUM, Rawtenstall

For such a small town as Rawtenstall this is an excellent museum and art gallery. The collection is housed at Oak Hill, an impressive Victorian mill owner's mansion in Whitaker Park, above the town. It was built in 1840 for local wool mill owner George Hardman, but in 1896 the house and twenty-eight acre estate was bought by Richard Whitaker, who was at one time an overlooker at the Hardman family's mill. He had made a fortune in Canada as a mill owner himself. At his own expense Whitaker transformed the Hardman estate into a attractive public park. He then presented the park and mansion to the Borough of Rawtenstall and the house opened as a museum in 1902. After such a magnificent gesture Whitaker was made a freeman of the borough. His golden freedom casket is on show in the museum.

The interesting collection includes fine and decorative art, local and social history and natural history. The big display of stuffed animals, birds and reptiles is popular with children. One room has been furnished as the Hardman family's sumptuous drawing-room. There are some excellent paintings in the museum with a gallery reserved for temporary art exhibitions.

The park features a small aviary and a pets' corner. Above the park is the Rossendale dry ski slope, which also has a cafe.

Location: Haslingden Road, near town centre.

Opening times: April-October - Monday to Friday 1.00 pm to 5.00 pm. Saturday 10.00 am to 5.00 pm. Sunday noon to 5.00 pm. November-March - Monday to Friday 1.00 pm to 5.00 pm. Saturday 10.00 am to 4.00 pm. Sunday noon to 4.00 pm.

Telephone: 01706 226590.

Partial disabled access only.

WEAVERS' COTTAGE, Rawtenstall

The three-storey Weavers' Cottage was built in 1780 for hand loom weaving. Exhibits inside include a clogger's shop and a Victorian kitchen.

Location: In the centre of Rawtenstall.

Opening times: Every Saturday and Sunday, 2.00 pm to 5.00 pm.

Telephone: 01706 229937.

No specific disabled access.

The end of the line. Rawtenstall station, terminus of the East Lancashire Railway.
Hugh Thom

LAMBERT HOWARTH FOOTWEAR MUSEUM, Rawtenstall

The Footwear Museum shows aspects of the Rossendale Valley's once great shoe and slipper industry. The Museum was set up by Lambert Howarth, shoe manufacturers, who own factories at Burnley and Rawtenstall. The Museum and mill shop are at the Rawtenstall factory, which is near the town centre, having been moved there from Waterfoot.

Location: Fall Barn Road, Greenbridge. (near the Asda store)
Opening times: Monday to Friday 9.30 am to 5.00 pm. Saturday 9.00 am to 4.00 pm, Sunday, 10.00 am to 4.00 pm.
Telephone: 01706 215417.
Full disabled access available.

IRWELL SCULPTURE TRAIL

A walk along the Irwell Valley Way from Bury to Stacksteads through Ramsbottom and Rawtenstall allows a view of works of art beside the river as well as the grand scenery. The Irwell Sculpture Trail is claimed to be the largest public art scheme in Britain. More than fifty artists have been commissioned to design sculptures to place alongside the river Irwell.

The scheme has a budget of £4.2 million. Further sculptures are to be installed between Salford and Bury. The Irwell Valley Way is a well-established footpath that stretches for thirty miles from the Salford quays into the Rossendale valley.

Leaflets describing and pinpointing the position of the sculptures can be obtained from local Tourist Information Centres.

Runcorn and Widnes

HALTON CASTLE, Runcorn

One of only two Norman castles in Cheshire, Halton Castle was built on the edge of a crag which overlooks Runcorn. The sandstone outer walls are still intact and enclose a large grassed area, but at the time of writing no-one was allowed inside.

The impressive Castle Hotel is built into the walls, and once housed the Castle's Law Courts. The castle walls are near the edge of a precipice, but there is a safe footpath right round the outside of the castle, giving the walker a spectacular view over the Manchester Ship Canal and adjacent river Mersey to Widnes on the other side. The stupendous arched Runcorn-Widnes road bridge looks like a toy in the near distance.

Halton Castle was built of sandstone quarried on Runcorn Hill around 1134. After the Norman Conquest, an earlier castle was constructed on this site around 1070. It was simply a ditch surrounding a wooden stockade.

Halton Village, now a conservation area, is the oldest part of Runcorn, and is well worth walking round. It is dotted with old sandstone homes, including a Tudor mansion near the castle which was once occupied by the Castle Sheriff.

Runcorn may be famous for its chemical works, but Halton village and neighbouring Runcorn Hill are charming places high up and away from industry.

Refreshments may be obtained at the Castle Hotel or at the nearby *Norton Arms* at the bottom of The Underway.

RUNCORN HILL NATURE RESERVE

Runcorn Hill, with its woodland walks and heathland, was once the site of a huge sandstone quarry, the busiest and largest in Cheshire. Quarrying here dates back to 1734. A leaflet describing a one hour Quarry Trail walk can be obtained from the Visitor Centre at Highlands Road. Stone for the building of the Bridgewater Canal was quarried here.
Telephone: 01928 560793. (Visitor Centre)

Runcorn-Widnes Road Bridge: A striking view of the Runcorn-Widnes road bridge. (Runcorn's answer to the Sydney Harbour Bridge) can be enjoyed near the Ship Canal and adjoining river

Mersey at Mersey Road. There are seats on the grass 'promenade' here.

CRONTON AND PEX HILL COUNTRY PARK, near Widnes
The picturesque village of Cronton, near Widnes, and nearby Pex Hill Country Park can be combined into one visit. Cronton, a substantial village, is a mile south of the M62 as it approaches the Merseyside region. It features many seventeenth and eighteenth century buildings with Cronton Hall as the centrepiece. The village stocks are unusual in having five holes instead of the usual four. The small Pex Hill Country Park is moorland which offers excellent views.
Location: Cronton is on the A5080 north of Widnes and near Junction 7 of the M62.
Opening times: The Visitor Centre is open on Saturdays and Sundays.

Salford

SALFORD QUAYS AND LOWRY CENTRE

One of the most exciting tourist places in Greater Manchester is Salford Quays, site of the former Manchester Docks which geographically were in Salford.

Here, beside the Manchester Ship Canal, has risen the fabulous Lowry Centre which opened to the public in April, 2000. The centre has been built to display the world's largest collection of paintings and drawings by Salford artist L.S. Lowry, along with the Lowry Study Centre. There is a 1,650 seat theatre suitable for world class performances of opera, ballet and drama and a 400-seat theatre for local groups. The Lowry Centre also contains Britain's first children's hands-on gallery, enabling young people to experience all aspects of the world of the arts.

The Lowry collection was moved from Salford Art Gallery to the Lowry Gallery at Salford Quays, but free admission continues. Unfortunately only a portion of the Lowry collection is on view at any one time.

The Lowry building was voted as Britain's outstanding building for 2001. From a distance it looks a little like a collection of tin cans as the façade of the building is faced with steel. Inside an escalator

The new footbridge over Salford Quays between The Lowry Centre and the Imperial War Museum. The bridge can be raised to allow ships to pass underneath.
Ted Birch

The steel clad Lowry Centre at Salford Quays. David Hollows

The tower of the steel clad Lowry Centre at Salford Quays. David Hollows

takes one up to the plain whitewashed art galleries (the two theatres are on the ground floor). Outside a dramatic white footbridge spans the Manchester Ship Canal. It has towers featuring lifting equipment so that the bridge can be lifted to allow ships to pass underneath. On the other side of the Ship Canal, in the borough of Trafford, is the Imperial War Museum North, another dramatic building which is due to open in July, 2002 (see Trafford chapter for details regarding the Imperial War Museum North).

A walk round Salford Quays is a real pleasure, as there is much to see, including attractive waterside housing and dramatic glass walled office blocks. There is a big quayside pub serving full meals. In the early 1980s the Salford Quays site lay derelict after being used for more than ninety years as a busy port. A development plan, published in 1985, set out proposals to create an area in which people could live, work and play. The site was transformed with extensive tree planting. Quayside boulevards with attractive lighting columns systems and street furniture were developed. And the filthy dock basins have been transformed into clear water areas in which fish live. What an achievement!

Location: Salford Quays is on Trafford Road, between the A56 at Old Trafford and the M602 at Salford.

Full disabled access available at the Lowry Centre.

A spectacular office building at Salford Quays. Ken Matthews

SALFORD MUSEUM AND ART GALLERY, Peel Park, The Crescent

The impressive Salford Museum and Art Gallery has achieved special fame because it possessed the world's largest public collection of the paintings and drawings of the Salford artist, L.S. Lowry (1887-1976). The 200-item collection filled a substantial gallery and the imaginative display gave insights into the artist's life, with interesting biographical captions to his work. The Lowry Collection has now been moved to The Lowry Centre at Salford Quays. 'Very, very few people liked my work', said the eccentric lifelong bachelor. He realised, however, that artists had ignored Britain's industrial landscape, so he made a name for himself by filling the gap.

Lowry spent thirteen years attending Salford School of Art and worked as a rent collector and clerk, painting in the evenings. He sold few paintings but was given his first solo exhibition in London in 1939, followed in 1941 by a major exhibition at Salford Museum and Art Gallery. But it was only after his retirement in 1952 that his fame really grew. The success of the Matchstalk Men record made him one of few artists to be immortalised by the music industry.

LARKHILL PLACE

Despite losing The Lowry collection, Salford Museum and Art Gallery has much to offer. It has an elegant gallery of splendid Victorian oil paintings and stages excellent temporary exhibitions in another large gallery.

In the basement is Larkhill Place, where old shop fronts from an area of Salford close to the gallery have been assembled to form a street scene with cobbled roadway, gas lamps, horse-drawn carriages and penny farthing bicycles. It is fascinating to peep into the shop windows and see goods that were sold in Victorian or Edwardian times. There is a blacksmith's workshop, a pawnbroker's, toy shop, pub, clogger, antiquated chemist and a door bearing a plaque which reads, 'Mrs Driver, bleeder with leeches'. The house of a rich family contrasts with the cottage of a poor man. No doubt most of Manchester and Salford's children are taken to see this wonderful street.

Location: On the A6 next to Salford University. The stone façade of the Art Gallery backs onto Peel Park and the river Irwell (There is a good walk here).

Opening times: Monday to Friday 10.00 am to 4.45 pm. Saturday, Sunday, 1.00 pm to 5.00 pm. Cafe.

Telephone: 0161 736 2649.

Full disabled access available.

SALFORD CATHEDRAL, Salford

This Roman Catholic Cathedral, opened in 1848, is an impressive site with its walls and wonderful spire dressed in buff coloured stone. Pleasant garden and book shop in courtyard.

Location: Chapel Road (A6).

Opening times: Open to the public from Monday to Friday between the 8.00 am and 12.10 pm Masses.

Telephone: 0161 834 0333.

BARTON AERODROME, near Eccles

Visitors are welcome at Barton Aerodrome, home of the Lancashire Aero Club, Britain's oldest flying club. It is a good place to watch light aircraft in flight as about 100 planes are based here. The visitor centre houses a free entry museum containing interesting relics and photographs of the Royal Air Force during the Second World War. The museum is described as 'great place to wallow in nostalgia'. There are wax figures wearing Battle of Britain Fighter Command and Luftwaffe uniforms.

The history of the Lancashire Aero Club (formed in 1922) is described in words and pictures. The museum is open from 10.00 am to 4.30 pm every Saturday and Sunday from April to October, and Sundays only in winter. It is open seven days a week during school summer holidays.

A major contribution to the displays is from the Macclesfield Historical Aviation Society that moved to Barton in 1994. The society has a workshop here for the restoration of vintage aircraft, to which the public is admitted.

For a dramatic view of aircraft landing or taking off go to the Eccles end of the airfield by walking or driving along the A57. You can then walk across grassland between the airfield perimeter fence and a line of trees. The planes usually come in to land over these trees and over your head. From here there is a rectangular walk around the airfield along a footpath, then a lane, bringing you back to the A57, along which one walks back to the airfield entrance.

The Lancashire Aero Club has around 400 members and some planes are owned - like racehorses - by syndicates. The club originally used the airfield at Woodford in Cheshire but switched to Barton in 1948. The airfield at Barton opened in 1930 and in 1936 became what was intended to be Manchester's international airport. But it was soon found to be inadequate, so Manchester City Council had a re-think and instead developed its vast airport at Ringway.

The control tower at Barton is the oldest in Britain and this and

one of its original hangars are listed buildings.
Location: Airfield entrance on A57 Eccles to Warrington road. Cafe at visitor centre.
Telephone: 0161 789 1866.
Full disabled access available at the Museum.

ORDSALL HALL, ORDSALL LANE, Salford

In the prosaic surroundings of council houses and factories in Salford's Ordsall Lane stands one of the best examples of Tudor architecture in the North of England. Ordsall Hall is a gem. It has a great hall which was built by Alexander Radclyffe in 1512 to replace an earlier cruck hall. A tiny door in a corner of the attractive hall opens into the Star Chamber bedroom with its gold stars on the ceiling, canopied bed and exposed wattle and daub section of wall. Another ground floor room is fitted out as a Victorian farmhouse kitchen and two rooms upstairs are used as a museum with temporary exhibitions about local history.

Admission is free to this half-timbered, medieval hall that was bought by Salford Corporation in 1959 and restored at great cost from semi-dereliction and opened to the public in 1972. The hall, in grounds now partly occupied by a car park, was once moated. The rest of Ordsall Hall, brick built at later dates, is not open to the public.

Once a month – on Sunday afternoons – the Living History Group, wearing period costume, give dramatised accounts of life at Ordsall Hall in Tudor times. Ring the hall on 0161 872 0251 to confirm dates.
Location: Trafford Road runs past Salford Quays from Old Trafford to the M602 at Salford. Ordsall Lane runs from Trafford Road's southern section to Ordsall Hall.
Opening times: Monday to Friday 10.00 am to 12.30 pm and 1.30 pm to 5.00 pm. Sunday 2.00 pm to 5.00 pm. Closed Saturday.
Partial disabled access only.

BLACKLEACH COUNTRY PARK, Walkden

The existence of the 100-acre Blackleach Country Park is a tribute to those Walkden people who campaigned for years against a plan by British Coal, the landowners, to drain and fill in the large Blackleach Reservoir and use it for housing development. Salford City Council eventually bought the land, part of which was badly scarred by a dye works and colliery spoil heaps, the industrial dereliction was removed and the country park became a glorious reality in 1995.

Centrepiece of the park is Blackleach Reservoir, which looks like a natural lake. It used to supply water to the network of underground coal transport canals which linked the Duke of Bridgewater's pits to his Bridgewater Canal at Worsley. Plenty of wildfowl can be seen here and there is angling which has been enjoyed for more than a century. The rest of the park consists of open land and woodland where volunteer workers have planted a lot of trees. An old colliery railway line used to run through this land – now it is a footpath which runs to Worsley.

Location: The park is just off Bolton Road (A575), half a mile north of Walkden shopping centre. Turn off Bolton Road into Hill Top Road, then into John Street to the car park.

Telephone: 0161 790 7746.

CLIFTON COUNTRY PARK

Clifton Country Park lies on the west bank of the river Irwell as it flows from Kearsley to Clifton Junction. From the park's visitor centre walkers can get a leaflet about the Wet Earth Trail which focuses on the mining heritage of the former Wet Earth Colliery, so called because the mine flooded due to a leak caused by a geological fault from the Irwell.

An engineer, James Brindley, developed an ingenious system to remove water from the mine, which was opened in the early 1700s but closed for good in 1928.

Clifton Country Park features a large lake which was created through gravel extraction for the construction of the nearby M62.

Location: Approach from both north and south along the Manchester to Bolton Road (A666). Turn into Clifton House Road, right down Doe Brow and under the railway bridge.

Opening times: The visitor centre opens at 1.00 pm every day.

WORSLEY AND WORSLEY WOODS

At historic Worsley is one of the most photographed views in northern England, where the famous black and white Packet House is mirrored in the orange water of the Bridgewater Canal. The canal water is so coloured because of iron ore which seeps out of the amazing underground canals to the long since closed coal mines to the north of Worsley village.

The man responsible for the building of the Bridgewater Canal to carry coal to Manchester was Francis Egerton, third Duke of Bridgewater, and owner of the mines. In Worsley village centre you can see the rock face from which the underground canal section emerged. There were forty-six miles of canals between the various pits. Coal boats were pushed by hand pressure on rails on the tunnel

The Bridgewater Canal at Worsley village. Ken Matthews

walls. Some tunnels were 550 feet below the surface.

James Brindley, who could neither read nor write, was the engineer of the Bridgewater Canal, which started our modern transport system. The aqueduct he built over the river Irwell was a wonder of the age (it was replaced by the present swing bridge at Barton when the Manchester Ship Canal was opened). The canal from Worsley to Manchester was completed in 1764 and the route through Cheshire to Runcorn in 1776.

Members of the Egerton family once lived at Worsley Old Hall which is now a restaurant. Turn up the Walkden road to get to the lane which leads to the Hall. At the canal in Worsley there are always many attractive narrow boats.

From Worsley, a lane leads past cottages to the hidden Worsley Woods. The path continues by a lake and eventually under the motorway, then beside a stream to the lovely village of Roe Green.

There is a cafe at Worsley Hall Garden Centre, half a mile from Worsley Village. The garden centre occupies the former walled garden of Worsley New Hall, a massive mansion which was demolished after the Second World War.

Southport

SOUTHPORT BOTANIC GARDENS AND MUSEUM

One would expect a classy resort like Southport to possess an outstanding park. You will not be disappointed if you visit the Botanic Gardens and Museum at Churchtown.

These outstanding gardens need most of half a day to see everything. The splendidly landscaped gardens include a beautiful boating lake with a brook running in and out of it on its way to the Ribble Estuary. Swans and ducks complete the picture and the gardens are inhabited by red squirrels. There is a glasshouse fernery, an aviary and a cafe. The gardens are sectioned by trees and hedges so there are surprises around corners.

The museum, which is Southport's only one apart from the National Museum of Lawnmowers (that's in a local shop) was purpose built in 1876. It includes a new gallery called 'Southport Seaside Garden City', which traces the first 200 years of the town's history. Other sections of the museum include the Victorian Room, featuring displays of nineteenth century life, the Pennington Collection of stuffed British birds and a display of Victorian and more modern toys.

Admission was not always free to the gardens and museum. It was founded in 1874 and built up as a commercial venture by a group of local men. In 1932 the company failed and the land, museum and contents were sold by auction. Southport Corporation bought the site and buildings in 1936 from a private developer to prevent homes being built there.

Location: Botanic Road, Churchtown, at the northern tip of Southport. Churchtown is a picturesque and historic village and the Churchtown Village Trail guide can be obtained at the Museum.

Opening times: Museum: Tuesday to Friday 11.00 am to 3.00 pm, Saturday, Sunday 2.00 pm to 5.00 pm. Monday closed (but open Bank Holiday Mondays and closed the following Fridays).

Telephone: 01704 227547.

Partial disabled access only.

ATKINSON ART GALLERY, Lord Street, Southport

Southport has always been famous for Lord Street, with its elegant arcaded shops. What better site could there be for the impressive Atkinson Art Gallery.

The main strengths of the permanent collection, which started in 1879, are eighteenth and nineteenth century English watercolours and British paintings just before and after the 1900s. There is a small collection of British contemporary paintings, sculptures and prints.

An ever changing programme of temporary exhibitions includes the work of Southport Palette Club and Southport Photographic Society.

Opening times: Monday, Tuesday, Wednesday and Friday 10.00 am to 5.00 pm. Thursday and Saturday, 10.00 am to 1.00 pm. Closed Sunday and Bank Holidays.

Telephone: 0151 934 2110.

Full access for disabled.

SOUTHPORT PIER

Southport Pier, the second longest pier in Britain at just under one mile, has been closed to the public for several years because of its unsafe state. However, it is now being re-built, partly financed by various grants that were given on condition that the pier remains a free admission attraction.

'Traumatizer', the tallest and fastest suspended looping roller coaster in the United Kingdom, at Southport's Pleasureland. It pulls over 4+G and reaches speeds of 85 k.p.h.

I was originally told that it was due for re-opening in September 2001, but this massive re-building scheme seems to have run into difficulties, for at the time of writing (January 2002), there was still no sign of completion. Hopefully it will be open again before too long.

Built in 1860, the pier is the oldest in Britain. There were no amusements on it but the re-building plan includes a Heritage Centre, restaurant and bar at the sea end. The pier starts on the promenade and crosses the Marine Lake before continuing over the sands. The old pier railway was removed when the pier closed but a new railway is envisaged for the re-built structure.

RED SQUIRREL RESERVE, Freshfields, Formby
The National Trust may be best known for looking after stately homes, but at Formby it does one of its most important jobs – preserving beautiful stretches of our coastline. Here it owns 500 acres of beach, foreshore and sand dunes and in the pinewoods live a colony of 250 to 300 red squirrels. Many sightings of these beautiful but rare animals are guaranteed as you walk in the woods. And from the squirrel reserve visitors can walk down to the beach

A red squirrel at the squirrel reserve in Formby. Heather Bradshaw

along a well defined track, passing dunes and heathland. It is a peaceful and lovely place.

People may walk into the nature reserve free, but there is a substantial fee for cars in the National Trust car park. Many will pay this willingly as a donation to the Trust, but if you wish to avoid paying you can park in the Victoria Road area (the road leads down to the reserve from Freshfield railway station).

Formby is an upmarket residential town between Southport and Liverpool. From Freshfield you can walk north along the beach to Ainsdale and there catch a train back to Freshfield. They run frequently.

Facilities: There are toilets at the nature reserve.
Telephone: 01704 878591.

MERE SANDS WOOD NATURE RESERVE, near Rufford
This nature reserve comprises more than 100 acres of lakes, heath and coniferous woods and contains a wealth of wildlife.
Location: Immediately west of Rufford, on B5246. Rufford is eight miles east of Southport's Marine Lane as the crow flies. A mile away from Mere Sands Nature Reserve are the pleasant grounds of Ruffold Old Hall. There is an admission charge for the house.

Stockport

PEAK FOREST CANAL LOCKS, Marple

The Peak Forest Canal runs through hilly Marple via a remarkable series of sixteen locks. These are in good working order and the walk along this stretch of canal is, consequently, very interesting. The locks are on either side of the A626 from Stockport, which plunges down to Marple Bridge. South of the A626 the canal runs through a picturesque stretch of the town to its junction with the Macclesfield Canal where there is always a colourful display of boats. North of the A626 the canal crosses the river Goyt on a viaduct passing under the higher railway viaduct and giving a spectacular view. The beautiful Marple area is an excellent centre for walking.

Location: Four miles east of Stockport town centre.

BROOKSIDE GARDEN CENTRE AND MINIATURE RAILWAY, Macclesfield Road, Poynton

Six engines, some steam, some diesel, take passengers on a 760-yards ride through the landscaped grounds from an authentic GWR country station festooned with railway signs from all parts of the country. There is a small museum, a full size signal box, a tunnel and

The miniature railway at Brookside Garden Centre, near Stockport.

two rail bridges over Norbury Brook. Volunteer railway buffs have built up and operate this nostalgic line. The 50p fare goes to children's charities. Trains run every Saturday and Sunday throughout the year and seven days a week during July and August.

At Brookside Garden Centre children can also climb on the footplate of a full size tank engine. The centre also features a birds of prey section and a pottery kiln workshop where visitors are able to throw their own pots. There is a good restaurant. Go early on summer Sundays - in the afternoons it gets very busy.
Location: On A523 four miles south of Stockport.
Telephone: 01625 872919.

ETHEROW COUNTRY PARK, Compstall, near Stockport
This is one of the most beautiful country parks in the North West. It includes an old mill lodge feeder canal, the river Etherow, hilly woodlands and a hidden, tree-surrounded lake which nestles in the deep valley below rugged moors.

The country park starts at the village of Compstall on the B6104 between Romiley and Marple Bridge. The village was created by local industrialist George Andrew, who built the beautiful lodge next to which visitors park their cars. Andrew also built the feeder canal which receives water from the river Etherow.

Andrew's textile mill closed in 1966 and three years later 165 acres of the valley became one of Britain's first country parks. In 1986 a further eighty-one acres, at Ernocroft Wood, were acquired.

At the large lodge there are many types of geese and ducks. A path follows the feeder canal to the spectacular river weir up the valley. Then follows a pretty walk through The Keg woodlands with fine hill views and Keg Pool.
Facilities: Cafe and toilets at lodge car park.

STOCKPORT ART GALLERY, Wellington Road South
The full name for this attractive building near the town centre is Stockport War Memorial and Art Gallery. Part of the building's ground floor has walls covered with the names of local people who died in both world wars. The land was given to the town for the erection of a war memorial on condition that it was also used for educational purposes. Hence this unusually located art gallery which occupies the first floor and two small ground floor rooms.

There are constantly changing exhibitions, but only a fraction of Stockport's permanent art collection can be shown because of lack of space.

A train on the massive viaduct in Stockport town centre, with the bus station below.

Location: On A6 just south of town centre.
Opening times: Monday, Tuesday, Thursday, Friday, 11.00 am to 5.00 pm. Saturday 10.00 am to 5.00 pm. Closed Wednesday and Sunday.
Telephone: 0161 474 4453.
Partial disabled access only.

BRAMALL HALL PARK, Bramhall

Although there is an admission charge for Bramall Hall, its picturesque park is worth visiting alone. The local brook runs through the park and there is an attractive pool below the hall. The black and white Elizabethan east facade of the hall is a magnificent sight.

This park lies in the middle of a six-mile linear walk of great charm from Cheadle to Poynton Lake, nearly all of it along the Micker Brook which becomes Lady Brook to the east of Bramall Hall. Cars can be left at Cheadle and Poynton, so you can walk one way only between them.

Location: Bramall Hall Park is on the A5102, three miles from Stockport town centre. Cafe behind Bramall Hall.

Stockport Museum, in Vernon Park. Elisabeth Rowlatt

STOCKPORT MUSEUM, Vernon Park

The museum covers the social and industrial history of the town. An outstanding exhibit is an 8 foot by 3½ foot window in Blue John fluorspar from Castleton. It was made and presented to the museum by former curator John Tymm, and is the largest known Blue John window. Stockport-born tennis champion Fred Perry is remembered here with a small display of memorabilia.

The museum has been enlarged with the opening of a 'times past in Stockport' section in the basement. The museum's location means

A replica of a Russian cannon captured during the Crimean War stands outside the museum in Vernon Park, Stockport.

that visitors can walk through adjoining parks (Vernon and Woodbank) along the bank of the river Goyt, as far as Marple if they feel energetic.

In the second half of 2000 Vernon Park was re-opened after £2M was spent on restoring it to its Victorian condition.

Location: Portwood, on the east side of the town centre.

Opening times: From 1 April to 31 October, the museum is open seven days a week, 1.00 pm to 5.00 pm. From 1 November to 31 March: Saturdays and Sundays only, 1.00 pm to 5.00 pm.

Telephone: 0161 474 4460.

No specific disabled access.

LYME PARK, Disley, near Stockport

There is a substantial entrance fee for cars at Lyme Park (£3.30 at time of writing) which is payable on arrival at the car park near Lyme Hall. But it is included because it is a great place for walkers, and there are several places around the perimeter of the park where cars can be left and walking is free.

Lyme Park is a little on the wild side, because the moorland at the south end of the park rises to 1,200 feet. Visitors can enjoy the presence of the herd of red deer which are descendants of those that once roamed Macclesfield Forest. They have been at Lyme since the reign of Elizabeth I when the park was enclosed.

The red deer, which roam most of the park's 1,300 acres, numbered at least 400 at the time of writing. The animals are not tame and will not allow visitors to get too close. But if you walk the park in September or October you may see the bellowing stags fighting over the hinds as the mating season arrives. Lyme also supports about 100 fallow deer in a sanctuary behind the hall.

Lyme Hall and Park was owned by the Legh family for 600 years and is now managed by the National Trust, with financial support from Stockport Council. There is an excellent children's playground in a dell near the hall.

Location: Park main entrance on A6 Stockport-Buxton road.

Telephone: 01663 762023.

REDDISH VALE COUNTRY PARK, Reddish, near Stockport

This comparatively new country park covers a beautiful area of the Tame Valley north of Stockport. From the visitor centre at the bottom of the valley below Reddish there is a spectacular view across two mill lodges to an impressive sixteen-arch railway viaduct.

Swans and scores of other birds, including heron, use the lakes.

Ramblers can enjoy walking beside the river Tame as far as Denton or Hyde, or they can walk south to Stockport along a disused railway line.

You can drive to the visitor centre car park down Reddish Vale Road which starts near Reddish South railway station. The visitor centre, which is open every day between 10.00 am, and 4.00 pm, has plenty of space for wildlife exhibits and frequent displays of landscape paintings.

The textile mill buildings were erected in 1780 and demolished in 1997 (330 people were employed here in 1922). When the viaduct was built in 1875 it is said that a local witch who was opposed to the construction warned that anyone who counted the arches would have bad luck.

Location: (Visitor Centre) Reddish Vale Road, off B6167, two miles north of Stockport town centre.

BARTON GRANGE GARDEN CENTRE, Woodford

This is the most extensive of three Barton Grange garden centres (the others are at Bolton and Preston). This centre features landscaped grounds with ponds, trees, and winding paths. There is an aquatic and pets section and a restaurant.

Location: On Chester Road, Woodford (A5102) one mile south of Bramhall and opposite the British Aerospace factory.

Opening times: Monday to Saturday 9.30 am to 5.30 pm. Sunday 10.30 am to 4.30 pm.

Telephone: 0161 439 0745.

St Helens

PRESCOT MUSEUM, St Helens

For more than 300 years Prescot, a small town wedged between Liverpool and St. Helens, was noted for the manufacture of watch movements, clock components and the tools required for watch and clock making. So it is fitting that half the space in Prescot Museum is occupied by horological exhibits. On display is a traditional clockmaker's workshop of the type that was set up in Prescot and the surrounding villages. The museum also contains a gallery devoted to other aspects of Prescot history, while the ground floor is used for temporary exhibitions.

This museum, which is of national importance, occupies a handsome former bank building in Church Street, and was opened in 1982.

Watchmaking was established in the Toxteth area of Liverpool in the early 1600s, but the industry was concentrated in Prescot during the 1700s. By 1800 the town was the principal centre for the manufacture of watch movements and watch and clock components. However, in the last quarter of the nineteenth century the Americans and Swiss eclipsed the Lancashire industry. By the 1920s only a small number of the several hundred Prescot workshops survived and the last one closed in 1952. The Lancashire Watch Company set up a Prescot factory in 1890, but that had closed by 1909.

Location: On corner of Church Street and High Street. Near junction 2 of the M57.

Opening times: Wednesday to Saturday 10.00 am to 1.00 pm and 2.00 pm to 5.00 pm. Sunday 2.00 pm to 5.00 pm and Bank Holiday Mondays from 10.00 am.

Telephone: 0151 430 7787.

Partial disabled access only.

RAINFORD ART GALLERY, St Helens

The town's small art gallery is housed on the first floor of the Gamble Institute in Victoria Square.

Opening times: Monday to Saturday 9.30 am to 5.00 pm.

Telephone: 01744 456951. (Tourist information is also on this number).

Partial disabled access only.

SHERDLEY PARK, St Helens

The 300 acres of Sherdley Park include formal gardens and woodland walks. There is also a large children's play area. This Park is used to stage the St Helens Show, claimed to be the largest free show in the country. Sherdley Park and Sherdley Hall were once owned by Copper magnate Michael Hughes. Following his death in 1825 the estate fell into disrepair. It was bought by St Helens Corporation in 1949.
Location: Well south of the town centre at Marshalls Cross Road.
Telephone: 01744 815586.

ST MARY'S, LOWE HOUSE, CATHOLIC CHURCH, St Helens

This remarkable Catholic Church in the centre of St Helens boasts a massive green copper dome. Called the poor man's cathedral, St Mary's has an impressive square tower in the manner of Liverpool Cathedral. There is much to see inside St Mary's, the building of which was completed in 1928. It is faced with grey stone.
Location: North Road off Corporation Street.
Opening times: Restricted to before and after the various masses (usually between 11.30 am and 1.30 pm). Longer hours on Sundays. It is best to get there between 11.15 am and 11.30 am. If the church is shut call at the Presbytery in Crab Street, down one side of the church and they may open the church and show you around.
Telephone: 01744 22167.
Full disabled access available.

SANKEY VALLEY PARK, St Helens

I led a party of walkers along the Sankey Valley from Newton-le-Willows to Carr Mill Dam, which is a large lake beside the A580 East Lancs. Road at St Helens.

The Sankey Valley is an historic place, the scene of the building of the Sankey Navigation (1757), the first canal to be dug in England. Mersey Weaver flats, boats with sails, brought goods up the Mersey to Warrington and then up the Sankey Valley to St Helens. Coal thus reached Liverpool cheaply and copper ore was brought to a works at St Helens.

The walk is along the Sankey brook. Two sections of the canal, between Warrington and St Helens, are still there. This linear park between the East Lancashire Road and Newton-le-Willows is about three miles long. The Sankey Navigation was closed in 1963, ending 200 years of use. There is a Visitor Centre where the valley park crosses the A58 at St Helens.
Location: For a leaflet with a map, telephone the Rangers on 01744 815586.

Tameside

The Tameside local authority area to the east of Manchester includes the close-packed towns of Ashton-under-Lyne, Stalybridge, Hyde, Dukinfield and Droylsden and hilly Mossley to the north of the Tame Valley.

PORTLAND BASIN MUSEUM, Ashton-under-Lyne

This superb new free admission museum is housed in the rebuilt Ashton Canal warehouse built in 1834. It opened in 1999 and stands next to the canal basin at the junction of the Ashton and Peak Forest canals.

The highlight of the museum is its street of shops, church, schoolroom and public house which represent Tameside in the 1920s. The museum also contains intriguing working models of the Ashton Canal and a large floor housing exhibits about Tameside's many industries. Visitors can round off a pleasant day out with a walk along the nearby canals.

Portland Basin Museum, Ashton-under-Lyne. Elisabeth Rowlatt

Location: Portland Street South, in Ashton town centre, just south of Park Parade, the town's inner by-pass.
Opening times: Open all year, Tuesday to Sunday, 10.00 am to 5.00 pm.
Telephone: 0161 343 2878.
Full disabled access available.

ASTLEY CHEETHAM ART GALLERY, Stalybridge

This art gallery occupies the top floor of the library in Trinity Street, in the centre of Stalybridge. There are regular visiting exhibitions.
Opening times: Monday, Tuesday, Wednesday, Friday, from 1.00 pm to 7.30 pm. Saturday 9.00 am to 4.00 pm. Closed Thursday.
Telephone: 0161 338 2708.
No specific disabled access.

STALYBRIDGE COUNTRY PARK

This rugged moorland country park is a relatively new one, and at the time of writing was still being developed. The Brushes Valley with its four reservoirs became a protected area after plans to develop the lower part of the valley were beaten off.

Stalybridge Country Park includes a smaller area at Carrbrook, a mile to the north of the Brushes Valley, but the two areas are linked by moorland footpaths and lanes. The Brushes Valley starts at Walker Wood, just north of Stalybridge, and off the B6175 Stalybridge to Mossley Road. There is a visitor centre at Walker Wood. If you like reservoir walking in grand moorland scenery, then this is the place.

WERNETH LOW COUNTRY PARK, near Hyde

The crest of Werneth Low, a ridge between the towns of Hyde and Romiley, affords a spectacular view of the Hyde area. Motorists can drive up to Werneth Low from the B6014 at Romiley or from the A560 at Gee Cross in Hyde. There is both a cafe and a pub on top of the hill and a visitor centre.

The Etherow Country Park is a mile downhill from Werneth Low Country Park.

STAMFORD PARK, Ashton-under-Lyne

This is Tameside's main park, and very beautiful it is too. The setting is on different hillside levels, all screened by trees and shrubs. There are attractive formal flower gardens, a conservatory full of plants, pets' corner and bowling, tennis and crazy golf. At the top of the

park you can cross Darnton Road to a separate section featuring two large lakes.
Location: The park's main gate is on A635 Ashton to Stalybridge road.

FAIRFIELD MORAVIAN SETTLEMENT, Droylsden

The lovely cobbled streets of Georgian houses have been preserved to show the character of an eighteenth century Moravian community. The settlement is the largest of its kind in Britain and all the buildings have been listed as being of special architectural or historical interest. The streets are wide enough to accommodate trees in the centre.

The Moravian Church was an off-shoot of the first Protestant church in northern Europe. It was founded in Moravia, now part of the Czech Republic, in 1457 by people disenchanted with the Roman Catholic Church.

The English Settlement at Fairfield was founded in 1785. The church of that date is still a busy place with its own clergyman, who lives next door. The Moravians once had a theological college and boys' and girls' boarding schools here. The former theological college has been restored and turned into the settlement's Christian social centre.

If you wish to join one of the guided tours (small fee payable and limited to twenty) which are available from Easter to early September, book in advance by telephoning 0161 370 3461. Tea and biscuits included in the price.

In the Moravian graveyard small plaques, laid on the ground in regimented rows, mark the graves. Single men are buried on one side of the divided path and single women on the other. But married couples are allowed to share the same grave.
Location: The Moravian Settlement is three miles east of Manchester city centre. Fairfield Road is off Ashton Old Road (A635).

MUSEUM OF THE MANCHESTERS, Ashton-under-Lyne

The Queen Mother, a former Colonel-in-Chief of the Manchester Regiment, opened this excellent museum in Ashton Town Hall in 1987. Since then the museum has been greatly extended and includes video films of the two world wars and a research area with computerised equipment.

One interesting feature is a darkened cubicle which replicates night in a trench on the Western Front in 1917. Big guns boom, machine guns chatter and the sky over the top of the sandbags is lit up by exploding shells. The smell of the trenches is captured and soldiers crouch in the gloom.

The museum covers all the major conflicts in which the Manchesters were involved, plus a section about women in wartime. The Manchester Regiment was formed in 1881 and based at Ashton's former Ladysmith Barracks. The name ceased to exist in 1958 when the Manchesters were amalgamated with The King's Regiment (Liverpool). It is now known as the King's Regiment.

Opening times: Monday to Saturday, 10.00 am to 4.00 pm.

Telephone: 0161 342 3078.

Note: In the square outside Ashton Town Hall is a big daily open-air market.

Full disabled access available.

CENTRAL ART GALLERY, ASHTON-UNDER-LYNE

This gallery opened in 1998 and is on the first floor of Ashton's main library in Old Street, in the town centre. The gallery has no permanent collection but stages touring exhibitions and the work of local artists.

Opening times: Tuesday, Wednesday, Friday 10.00 am to 5.00 pm. Thursday, 1.00 pm to 7.30 pm.

Saturday 9.00 am to 4.00 pm. Closed Monday.

Telephone: 0161 342 2650.

Full disabled access available.

Trafford

IMPERIAL WAR MUSEUM NORTH

This impressive museum was due to open in 2002, hopefully by July. At the time of writing the spectacular building was under construction beside the Manchester Ship Canal, next to Salford Quays. It is on the Trafford Borough bank of the Ship Canal and is linked to The Lowry Theatre and Arts Centre by a rather spectacular white footbridge over the Ship Canal.

There is free admission for everyone to the Imperial War Museum North.

Location: Trafford Wharf Road, on the boundary between Trafford Borough and Salford.

Opening times: Yet to be fixed but the Museum will be open seven days a week.

Telephone: 0161 873 8598 or telephone Salford Tourist Information Centre on 0161 848 8601.

Restaurant.

Full disabled access available.

TRAFFORD CENTRE

The expressions on the faces of the many visitors who viewed the splendours of the Trafford shopping and leisure centre on the day it opened to the public in 1998, said it all. They were obviously delighted, even awed, at what they were seeing in the main shopping mall.

White figures adorn the columns at the Trafford Centre.

The upper mall of the Trafford Centre at Urmston.

The Orient at the Trafford Centre, with its changing skies ceiling.

The outside of the centre near Urmston is a stunning sight, thanks to its facing of golden stone and its three domes. Yet architects had already criticised the centre's classical style as not being original, but merely a throwback to Greek and Roman culture. The Manchester Evening News said that there was something 'absurdly artificial' about the ornate decor.

Thank goodness for this throwback, I say. The classical tradition in architecture, sculpture and art has remained popular throughout the centuries because it is surely the most noble and inspiring of all. There is nothing wrong with copying that.

With its lashings of gold leaf, fountains, murals, sculptures, classical columns, superb marble and granite flooring and huge mummified palm trees, the Trafford Centre is like a stately home for shoppers. It is designed to be a great day out as well as a shopping experience.

Even on the first floor galleries, one is a long way from the enormous glass roof. With the sun streaming down onto the marble floors visitors can imagine they are still outdoors. The natural light and filtered air prevents that feeling of claustrophobia which many experience in some shopping centres.

Without entering any of the 280 shops, restaurants and bars you can spend more than an hour exploring this vast complex. People with young children may be wise to leave them in the playroom or crèche if they want an aggravation-free tour.

The main dome of the Trafford Centre is claimed to be bigger than the dome of St Paul's Cathedral. The cream-coloured stone that decorates the building's exterior reminds one of Cotswold villages. On a high stone colonnade outside the building nude classical female figures play trumpets.

Inside the centre a highlight is the Orient Restaurant and Entertainment City. There is a 1,600 seat dining area under an amazing sky effect ceiling that changes from day to night, when thousands of 'stars' come out. There are world theme areas such as Chinatown and New Orleans. Also on site is a twenty-screen cinema complex and a bowling alley.

At the time of writing there are free admission weekly tea dances at the Trafford Centre. The dances, featuring a live band, take place on Tuesdays from 4.30 pm to 7.00 pm in the Orient dining area and include free coffee.

Note: Ladies should wear sensible shoes as the marble floor in the main mall is slippery. Go early if you go on Sunday as the approach roads to the Centre are gridlocked on Sunday afternoons.

Location: Near Urmston, between Junctions 9 and 10 of the M60.
Opening times: Trafford Centre shops Monday to Friday 10.00 am to 9.00 pm. Saturday 9.00 am to 7.00 pm. Sunday Noon to 6.00 pm. Restaurants are open to midnight, cinema to 3.00 am. (Sunday - midnight).
Full disabled access available.

DUNHAM PARK, near Altrincham

This vast tree-filled park is a favourite Sunday afternoon outing for people from south Manchester. The 10th Earl of Stamford, Roger Grey, was a confirmed bachelor and he bequeathed Dunham Massey Hall, the park with its herd of fallow deer and his estates to the National Trust when he died in 1976.

Dunham Park is included in this book because there is no admission charge to the park, although you have to pay to see the hall and gardens. Visitors can enjoy a meal in a charming restaurant in the stable block and sometimes there are art exhibitions in an adjoining room. Nearby, at the end of the moat, is a quaint Elizabethan water mill dating from 1616. The restored machinery is operated occasionally.

Winter at Sale Water Park, Borough of Trafford. Elisabeth Rowlatt

A short walk from the hall brings one to the river Bollin bridge. The peaceful hamlet here includes the *Swan with Two Necks* public house. A circular walk can include a section of the Bridgewater Canal.

Location: Dunham Park is on Charcoal Road, just off the A56 and 1¹/₂ miles from Altrincham town centre. There is a charge at hall car park.

Note: A section of the park is usually out of bounds to visitors to give the deer some privacy. While the deer often congregate in view of the public near the hall, the untimely deaths of some deer have been put down to stress because of the volume of visitors.

SALE WATER PARK, Sale

On a fine summer Sunday this lake near the river Mersey looks like a seaside resort. Hundreds of visitors sit on the sloping grass bank near the Trafford Watersports Centre and watch the intrepid users of yachts, water skis, jet skis, canoes and sailboards.

Bathers splash about in the shallow end, although swimming is not encouraged and anglers ply the quiet spots away from the madding crowd. The lake was created after contractors had excavated a half-mile long hole to build the embankment of the nearby motorway. The lake has a maximum depth of 90 ft.

The water park was officially opened in 1980 and now includes a waterside leisure centre with restaurant, licensed bar and changing rooms. Water sports gear can be hired here. At the south end of the lake there is a warden run information centre. Between the lake and the River Mersey is a wetland nature reserve with a hide.

The walk around the lake can be finished off along the river to the *Jackson's Boat* pub, a favourite outdoor drinking spot in summer. The footbridge over the Mersey here was once a private toll bridge. The pub's name is a reference to a man named Jackson who operated a ferry boat before the bridge was built.

Location: Sale Water Park lies between the towns of Sale and Stretford, just off the M60 ring road.

VICARAGE BOTANICAL GARDENS, Manchester Road, Carrington

The Vicarage Botanical Gardens at Carrington, two miles south of the suburban sprawl that is Urmston, is an oasis of peace and beauty in an industrial area.

Visiting the tree-surrounded gardens brings you to a 'secret world' and you forget the industrial structures on the skyline all around outside as they vanish from sight. The Christian community of eleven people here have created a lovely mini-world that includes herbaceous borders, a rose garden, woodland walks and, in season, rhododendrons galore. The work to produce this seven and a half acres site started in 1987.

The Anglican chapel here has been closed for several years, having served as a chapel of ease since it was built in 1872. One of the Earls of Stamford gave the chapel, the attractive Vicarage and the land to the Church of England. Eventually the Church gave the site back to the Stamford Estates and for eighteen years it was rented by Tony Mann of Round the World yacht race fame before the Christian community took over.

There is a small cafe and toilets at the Botanical gardens.

Location: On A6144 half a mile north of Partington.

Opening times: Saturday and Sunday 10.00 am to 6.00 pm. Weekdays 10.00 am to 12.30 pm and 1.30 pm to 5.00 pm. Closed Thursdays.

Telephone: 0161 775 2730 or 775 3679.

TRAFFORD PARK HERITAGE CENTRE

The Heritage Centre is next to St Anthony's Church at Trafford Park village. It features exhibitions about the vast industrial estate near Manchester. This area of factories was once the beautiful country estate of the De Trafford family.

Location: Third Avenue.

Opening times: Monday to Friday 9.00 am to 5.00 pm all year round.

Telephone: 0161 848 9173.

TRAFFORD ECOLOGY PARK

Also on the Trafford Park Industrial Estate, at Lake Road, is this green oasis in the midst of factories. There is a walk around what was once part of the lake at the long demolished Trafford Hall Nature Activities Centre here.

Location: Lake Road off Trafford Wharf Road.

Opening times: Monday to Friday 8.00 am to 5.30 pm (Summer).

Telephone: 0161 873 7182.

Warrington

WARRINGTON MUSEUM AND ART GALLERY

In 1998 there was a celebration of 150 years of collecting things at Warrington Museum and Art Gallery. And a new addition to the splendid collection was Chirotherium, the town's own breathing model dinosaur as well as a new geology gallery. Other galleries have been refurbished thanks to grants from the National Lottery.

Exhibits include Egyptology, Roman Britain, the Civil War, local industries, birds and mammals and glass. The building also houses a collection of around 1,000 paintings (oils, watercolours and prints) from the nineteenth and early twentieth centuries, some of which are on display in the mezzanine art gallery on the second floor. On the first floor there are two galleries for temporary exhibitions.

Location: Bold Street, in town centre.

Opening times: Monday to Friday 10.00 am to 5.30 pm. Saturday 10.00 am to 5.00 pm. Closed Sundays and Bank Holidays.

Telephone: 01925 442392.

Full disabled access available.

WARRINGTON TOWN HALL

Free evening tours of Warrington Town Hall can be arranged for parties of four or more. Set in parkland, this magnificent building was once the stately home of a copper smelting tycoon. The corporation bought it in 1873 and the interior still features paintings and fine furniture. The golden coloured wrought iron gates provide

The magnificent golden gates at Warrington Town Hall. Elisabeth Rowlatt

a sparkling entrance to the park.

To arrange tours telephone Warrington Town Hall on 01925 444400 or Warrington Tourist Information Centre on 01925 442180. Full disabled access available.

BURTON WOOD AIR FORCE BASE, near Warrington

Members of the Burtonwood Association have mounted a substantial free admission exhibition at the base about the famous site's history. This enormous RAF base, now shut down was occupied by the United States Air Force during the Second World War, when 18,000 Air Force and civilian personnel were involved at one time.

The nostalgic exhibition is in Unit 5 of the Header House, a gigantic wartime military warehouse. Five original wartime aircraft hangars are the only other important remains of the airbase. All war time aircraft were amazingly destroyed, one of the greatest pieces of vandalism ever. **Advice:** Visit now while admission is still free.
Location: Burtonwood Road, well northwest of Warrington, and north of the A57 Warrington to Liverpool Road. (Turn off A57 at Cromwell Avenue).
Opening times: Every Sunday from 2.00 p.m to 4.00 pm.
Telephone: 01925 725469.

LYMM, near Warrington

This attractive village with its famous pyramid of sandstone steps in

Lymm Cross. Elisabeth Rowlatt

the middle has a lake of rare beauty in Lymm Dam. It is surrounded by trees and is a place for romantics. A wooded path, in parts high above the water, takes you round the half mile long lake, ending at a narrow creek. At the dam end is the A56 Warrington road and if you cross this you can take another path which leads you into the centre of the village. From here a lane leads under the canal to a spectacular gorge with walls of rock plunging down to a stream.

At Lymm there are also pleasant walks along the Bridgewater Canal, and there is a public house, the *Golden Fleece*, with a canalside garden in the middle of the village.

RISLEY MOSS NATURE RESERVE, Warrington
Risley Moss is a special place – one of the few remaining damp mosslands in the British Isles. Peat was dug here for generations until the 1930s. The reserve offers a circular woodland walk of one mile from the impressive visitor centre. There is a high tower near the end of the walk with a grand view over the moss to the distant hills of Derbyshire.
Location: The Nature Reserve is one mile south of junction 11 on the M62. Take the A574 from the motorway roundabout and follow the Nature Reserve signs.

There are more woodland walks at nearby Birchwood Forest Park.

HIGH LEGH GARDEN CENTRE, near Lymm
Situated in lush Cheshire countryside, this big garden centre boasts massive indoor showrooms, including a general gifts department. Specialist demonstrations are given. It is open seven days a week throughout the year and there is a large cafe.
Location: At High Legh village, just off the Knutsford to Warrington road.
Telephone: 01925 756991.

WILLOW POOL GARDEN CENTRE, near Lymm
Just a mile away from High Legh garden centre is the eccentric but charming Willow Pool Garden Centre and Nursery. There is a picturesque pool and a collection of old bicycles and carts. The large showroom with antiques, paintings and furniture is well worth a visit. There is an excellent restaurant.
Location: Burford Lane, Lymm (on B5159 just north of Broomedge).
Opening times: From 9.00 am to 5.00 pm every day throughout the year.
Telephone: 01925 757827.

WALTON HALL GARDENS, Higher Walton, near Warrington

This big park is part of what used to be the private estate of the Greenall brewing family.

There is an interesting heritage centre with free admission which features pictures about life on the estate in the nineteenth and early twentieth century. Some of the estate's former splendour has been preserved with an array of shrubs and trees in the formal gardens. Of particular beauty are the rhododendrons and azaleas in spring.

The children's zoo is also free but what remains of Walton Hall is only open for weddings and private functions. The Hall was built in the Elizabethan style during the 1830s but much of it was demolished in the 1970s, being considered beyond repair.

Sir Gilbert Greenall became the first Lord Daresbury in 1927. His expertise in the breeding of horses and other livestock brought him international recognition and buyers came from many parts of the world to buy Walton stock. But his death in 1938 left the family owing £500,000 in death duties and the estate was sold by auction in 1941. Warrington Council bought part of it.

Facilities: Coffee shop in the heritage centre yard. The gardens are open all year from 8.00 am to dusk.

Location: Walton Lea Road, Higher Walton, just south of Warrington off the A56 (turn left at the *Walton Arms* public house). Gardens are two miles north of Junction 11 on the M56.

Telephone: For details of events in the park telephone the rangers on 01925 601617.

DARESBURY, near Warrington

This village was the birthplace of Lewis Carroll, author of *Alice in Wonderland*, whose real name was Charles Lutwidge Dodgson. He was the son of the Reverend Charles Dodgson, Vicar of Daresbury from 1827 to 1843, and he spent his childhood here.

There is a steady trickle of visitors from far and wide to All Saints Church which contains a stained glass window commemorating the centenary of the author's birth in 1832. The window depicts characters from his great book, including the Cheshire Cat. Special events were held at Daresbury in 1998 to mark the centenary of the author's death.

Location: Daresbury is south of Warrington and just north of Junction 11 of the M56. It lies alongside the A56, not far from Walton Hall Gardens.

Grappenhall village, near Warrington.

GRAPPENHALL, near Warrington

Grappenhall village is so near Warrington, yet nevertheless is a surprising paradise of peace and beauty. Good meals can be enjoyed at *The Parr Arms*, which stands in the charming cobbled street next to the ancient and rather magnificent Parish Church of St Wilfred. The church is open on Sunday afternoons in summer with parishioners to show you its treasures. The sandstone church has a thirteenth century medieval window among its notable stained glass.

There are lovely walks along the Bridgewater Canal, which runs through the centre of this upmarket village.

Location: Between Lymm and Stockton Heath on south side of the A56.

Wigan

HAIGH COUNTRY PARK, near Wigan

This is a country park with a stately home and private estate atmosphere. Haigh Hall itself is only used for private functions but the country park's cafe is to be found there.

The park's attractions, which bring couples with young families here in droves, include a model village, an excellent children's playground, a walled garden which is a riot of flowers in summer, and a miniature railway which takes passengers through the woods. There is also a craft gallery with a resident artist, crazy golf and woodland walks.

Both the Leeds and Liverpool Canal and the river Douglas cut through the park, which has an eighteen-hole golf course open to all. This is a beautiful place with more activities than at most country parks.

Location: Haigh Country Park is within easy reach of Junction 27 of the M6 or Junction 6 of the M61. From M6 turn east for Standish, then along B5239 to Haigh village. Haigh is about three miles northeast of Wigan town centre.

Telephone: 01942 832895.

WIGAN PARISH CHURCH

All Saints Church is one of the oldest churches in Lancashire, dating from the late Middle Ages. The present building was erected between 1845 and 1850. It is a lofty and well proportioned structure in the Perpendicular style. The lower part of the massive tower is thought to date from the thirteenth century.

Opening times: Beginning of May to end of September, every Saturday from 10.00 am to 4.00 pm. Guided tours if required.

Mondays and Wednesday, open for 12.30 pm services.

Location: Market Place, in the town centre.

Telephone: 01942 244459.

Full disabled access available.

PENNINGTON FLASH COUNTRY PARK, near Leigh

Pennington Flash, a mile-long lake, is at the centre of this country park in south Lancashire. It is regarded by many as the best bird watching territory in Greater Manchester. At least 200 different species have been recorded here.

Beside the lake, not far from the visitor centre and car park, lie

Wigan parish church.

several reed-fringed lagoons and ponds that teem with wildfowl and rarely seen birds. The country park offers interesting walks, including a four mile circuit of the flash. The lake was formed by subsidence due to extensive mine workings at the Bickershaw colliery. This interfered with drainage of the local brook and caused a massive build-up of water. A railway line ran across what is now the centre of the lake but closed in 1942 due to flooding.

Location: Drive along the East Lancashire Road (A580) from Manchester to its junction with the A579. Turn right here for Leigh and after one mile turn left along the A572 for the country park entrance.

TURNPIKE GALLERY, Leigh
This town centre Art Gallery occupies a large room above Leigh Library. Touring exhibitions and other exhibitions are usually changed every seven weeks or so.

Location: Next to the Town Hall in the Civic Square.

Opening times: Monday, Thursday, Friday, 9.30 am to 5.30 pm. Tuesday, 10.00 am to 5.30 pm. Wednesday, 9.30 am to 5.00 pm. Saturday, 10.00 am to 3.00 pm.
Telephone: 01942 404469.

ASTLEY GREEN COLLIERY MUSEUM, near Tyldesley

It is billed as Lancashire's last colliery and is managed by volunteers of The Red Rose Steam Society, a group of men who are in their element when they are tinkering with machinery.

Astley Green Colliery closed in 1970 because it was no longer economic to run. But what is Europe's largest steam winding engine remains and can still be seen in all its glory. The restored machinery is housed in a superb engine winding house which, with its arched windows, looks like an immense church. The pit headgear with its tower of latticed metal stands nearby.

The former pit lodge houses an exhibition about the colliery and its workers. Engines are in steam on the first Sunday of each month from March to October.

The pit village on either side of the Bridgewater Canal is an attractive place.

Astley Green Colliery Museum.

A stream flows down the ravine that is Borsdane Wood, between Westhoughton and Wigan. Kath Hodgson

Location: In Higher Green Lane, just off A580 (East Lancashire Road), signposted Higher Green, one mile from Boothstown.
Opening times: Sundays, Tuesdays, Thursdays, 1.00 pm to 5.00 pm all year round. Free admission except for special events.
Partial disabled access only.

BENTS GARDEN CENTRE, Warrington Road, Glazebury
Big garden centre, with extensive general gifts sections. Cafe. Open every day.
Location: On the A574 near its junction with A580 East Lancs Road, near Leigh.
Telephone: 01942 262066.

PARBOLD, NEWBURGH AND BEACON COUNTRY PARK

Parbold Hill, towering over the coastal plain to Southport, is a favourite stopping place for motorists on the A5209 for the dramatic views around them. And up the road from the *Wiggin Tree* pub-restaurant, on the top of Parbold Hill, is a footpath which plunges down the Fairy Glen, a wooded clough with impressive waterfalls after heavy rain, and many wild flowers.

Nestling below Parbold Hill are the attractive twin villages of Parbold and Newburgh which are well worth a stop and stroll around.

The Leeds and Liverpool Canal runs through Parbold village, where there is a station on the Wigan to Southport railway line. Two miles south of these villages is the Beacon Country Park, which consists of woodlands, meadows and pond areas. The park is on the slopes of Ashurst Beacon, and overlooks Skelmersdale. To get to the park from Newburgh turn up Higher Lane to Dalton Church, then turn left into Beacon Lane. On the other side of Beacon Lane to the country park is Ashurst Beacon, a stone monument which harks back to the beacons lit across England to warn of the approach of the Spanish Armada. From this high point you can see much of Lancashire. There is a visitor centre with bar and restaurant at Beacon Country Park.

Location: Parbold village is nearly four miles west of the M6 (Junction 27).

UP HOLLAND AND DEAN WOOD, near Wigan

The picturesque village of Up Holland, three miles west of Wigan, has cobbled streets and a fourteenth century parish church. In the sixteenth and seventeenth centuries it was a noted market town. After exploring the village you can take the two miles walk through the nearby Dean Wood. It is in a deep clough and follows Dean Brook as it flows to the river Douglas near the Gathurst viaduct of the M6. A group called the *Friends of Dean Wood* has improved footpaths with bridge building and board walks. A leaflet for walkers is available.

WORTHINGTON LAKES COUNTRY PARK, near Standish

This park is set in attractive countryside between Wigan and Adlington. Walks have been created round three reservoirs. Visitor Centre at the Worthington Reservoir.

Location: Chorley Road, Standish.
Telephone: 01257 425550.

The Wirral

HILBRE ISLAND

Hilbre Island lies a mile or so off the seafront at West Kirby. However, at low tide, it is sand all the way between the town and the island and it is a safe walk from the Wirral shore. It all makes for a fascinating day out for the long, thin island is a good place to watch seals, it is a noted bird sanctuary in the winter and there is an abandoned lifeboat station at one end. The sea is always right up on the outer side of the island which has high viewing points. There are no toilets on Hilbre.

However, be warned. You must start the walk and be back in West Kirby before the tide comes in! There are some days when it is inconvenient to walk to Hilbre because of the times of the tides. To check tides ring Wirral Country Park at Thurstaston (open 10.00 am to 5.00 pm) on 0151 648 4371 or 0151 648 3884. Staff will tell you that the walk from West Kirby marina to Hilbre should be via the tiny adjacent island of Little Eye because this is the safe, dry route but it is two miles out and two miles back. A map of the route, with tide times, is on display at West Kirby marina. For parties of ten walkers or more a permit to cross must be obtained.

PORT SUNLIGHT

Port Sunlight is a large but picturesque nineteenth century garden village on the Wirral built by the soap magnate William Hesketh Lever to house his workers in his factory there. It was named after

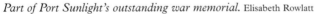

Part of Port Sunlight's outstanding war memorial. Elisabeth Rowlatt

The Lady Lever Art Gallery, Port Sunlight. Heather Bradshaw

Port Sunlight village, Wirral. Heather Bradshaw

The Dell at Port Sunlight village, Wirral. Bill Slater

his most famous product – Sunlight Soap. Even the village war memorial is fabulous. It is a mass of bronze figures in battle action, and must have cost a fortune.

If you call first at the heritage centre in Wood Street you can obtain a village trail leaflet. In the centre there is an exhibition about the village and William Hesketh Lever (later Lord Leverhulme) but there is a small admission charge.

The great glory of Port Sunlight is the magnificent Lady Lever Art Gallery which is open seven days a week. This treasure house was set up by the first Viscount Leverhulme in memory of his wife. The gallery contains masterpieces by Constable, Holman Hunt, Turner, Rossetti, and Burne-Jones as well as Chippendale furniture, sculptures and rare tapestries.

Up to 1997 admission to the art gallery was free, but then it was included in the £3 subscription scheme which gives entry for a year to Merseyside's top attractions. The over-sixties get a free pass however.
Location: Port Sunlight lies beside the Birkenhead to Chester road. (A41).
Opening times: Lady Lever Art Gallery – Monday to Saturday 10.00 am to 5.00 pm. Meals in Lady Lever Bistro.
Telephone: 0151 478 4136.
Full disabled access available.

GORDALE GARDEN CENTRE, SOUTH WIRRAL

This big garden centre near Burton has a vast indoor sales area with a range of gifts as well as house plants. There are peacocks in the garden and a coffee shop. The Waterworld fish and pets centre is less than 100 yards away.
Location: Seven miles from Chester on the A540, not far from Neston and the famous Ness Gardens.
Opening times: Monday to Saturday 9.00 am to 6.00 pm. Sunday 10.30 am to 4.30 pm.

WIRRAL COUNTRY PARK, THURSTASTON

Wirral Country Park is located along the former West Kirby to Hoole railway line and it includes part of the Wirral Way, a twelve miles long footpath along the former track. The country park affords splendid views across the Dee estuary to North Wales with access to the beach at various points. There is an excellent visitor centre at Thurstaston.
Location: Station Road, Thurstaston.
Telephone: 0151 648 4371.

EASTHAM COUNTRY PARK

This 100-acre country park is on the bank of the river Mersey on the Wirral between Port Sunlight and Eastham village. It occupies the site of former Victorian pleasure gardens and zoo and the bear pit and remains of ornamental fountains can still be seen.

The small park is mainly woodland and slopes gently down to the river affording visitors a splendid view to Liverpool Pier Head. The visitor centre, which has displays of local history, is open on Saturdays and Sundays, and in midweek when staff are there. In summer a tea garden is open but meals are always available at the *Eastham Ferry*, a pub beside the river.

The picturesque village of Eastham, a mile away, has sandstone cottages and a sandstone church with a great yew tree that is reputed to be a thousand years old. Eastham is where the Manchester Ship Canal joins the Mersey basin.

Location: Leave the M53 at Junction 5. Eastham Country Park is signposted from A41.

BRIMSTAGE HALL COURTYARD, BRIMSTAGE

Brimstage Hall, near Heswall, is a medieval pele or fortified tower at the hamlet of Brimstage in the centre of the Wirral. There are seven craft shops and a restaurant occupying part of the farm outbuildings and forming a courtyard.

They include The Voirrey Embroidery Centre, which has been featured on television. Here silks, wools, canvasses and kits cover all aspects of the needleworker's art. The upstairs gallery is used for new exhibitions monthly. Other craft shops display furniture, ceramics, ladies' clothing and gifts.

Location: Leave the M53 at Junction 4, driving one mile along the A5137 towards Heswall to Brimstage.

Opening times: Monday to Saturday 10.00 am to 5.00 pm. Sunday 1.00 pm to 5.00 pm.

Telephone: 0151 342 3514.

CHESHIRE OAKS, ELLESMERE PORT

Cheshire Oaks is described as a designer outlet village and consists of at least 150 shops and stores, restaurants and cafes.

Location: Kinsey Road, Ellesmere Port. Leave the M43 at Junction 10, one mile from the M53-M56 junction.

Opening times: Open seven days a week.

Telephone: 0151 357 3633.

Full disabled access available.

ROYDEN PARK AND THURSTASTON NATURE RESERVE

The wet heathland at Thurstaston Common, with its three types of heather, has been designated as a site of Special Scientific Interest. Thurstaston Hill is at the south end and Royden Park, with its visitor centre is at the north end. Royden Park includes a mere, walled garden, model railway, and a craft centre.

For good views walk to the top of Thurstaston Hill.

Location: Off the A450 near the Dee estuary, not far from West Kirby.

Opening times: The craft centre is open on Saturdays and Sundays only, May to October.

ARROWE COUNTRY PARK, near BIRKENHEAD
This 400-acre country park, a mixture of open land and deciduous woods, contains a golf course and pitch and putt course. The park, the largest on the Wirral, was once a private estate but has been publicly owned since 1928.
Location: Arrowe Park Road, Woodchurch, four miles west of Birkenhead town centre.
Opening times: The Visitor Centre is open every day. Wirral Council's garden nursery, at one end of the park is open to the public every Sunday from noon to 4.00 pm.
Telephone: 0151 666 5058 or 4371.

COURTS OF JUSTICE
Most large towns have daily sittings of Magistrates' Courts, and all of these provide seats for the public. An interesting day out can be spent sitting in these courts and watching a procession of defendants being dealt with from drunken drivers to thieves, rapists, burglars, armed robbers and the like.

These days comfortable tip-up seats are usually provided for spectactors, and most courts have their own cafes. My own local court, Trafford Magistrates Court at Sale, runs several court rooms simultaneously. So if you get bored with the proceedings in one court you can always switch to another court to see something more exciting.

Spectators are also welcome at the Crown Courts, which deal with the most serious cases and feature bewigged judges and barristers.

Other opportunities to watch people at work occur at the premises of big firms such as motor assembly plants, bakeries and breweries. Many of these guided tours are free but you usually have to book in advance, whereas you can just walk into any court room.

Free Annual Events

To find out the actual dates and times of this selection of free annual events, telephone the Tourist Information Centre that covers the town concerned (pages 189-191). While most of these events take place at the same time each year, the dates of a few may vary, so it is essential to check before setting out.

JANUARY
Late January: Battle of Nantwich. Colourful re-enactment of local Civil War battle, with Nantwich streets full of Roundheads, Cavaliers and other figures of the period. Normally held on Saturday closest to 25 January.

MARCH
Mid March (Sunday): St Patrick's Day parade in Manchester city centre. Part of the city's big Irish Festival.

APRIL
Mid April (Sunday): Sandbach Vintage Transport Parade through the town centre. *Highly recommended.*
Details on: 01270 873116.

Second weekend (Friday to Monday): Lancaster Easter Maritime Festival.

MAY
First Saturday in May: Knutsford Royal May Day parade. This is a quaint, charming carnival procession in which horse-drawn carriages predominate. Local children turn out in gorgeous costumes for the afternoon tour of the streets and on to Knutsford Heath for the crowning of the May Queen. There is a unique custom in which pictures are drawn in sand and dyed in many colours on the pavement outside the May Queen's house and on other pavements in town. Knutsford has an official sandman who carries out the work. A big funfair on the Heath completes Knutsford's big day.

First week (Bank Holiday Monday): Annual pet show in Moor Park, Preston. Family entertainment.

Early May (weekend): Merseyside's Open Houses. Free visits to Liverpool buildings usually closed to public.

Details on: 0151 708 8838.

Mid-May (Sunday): Southport Classic Cars Rally. Starts at 10.00 am from Floral Hall Gardens.

Mid-May: Lord Mayor's Parade at Chester (morning). An hour-long procession.

Mid-May (Saturday, Sunday): Chester Regatta on the river Dee.

Last week in May: Castleton (Derbyshire). Ancient Garland Ceremony with a procession round the village at 6.30 pm.

Last week in May (Bank Holiday Monday): Preston's Caribbean Carnival procession. (Moor Park, Deepdale Road).

Last week in May: Tideswell (Derbyshire) May Markets, with street entertainments.

JUNE
First Sunday: Morecambe and Heysham Carnival. Procession from promenade (late morning).

First Saturday: City of Liverpool Lord Mayor's Parade in city centre. **Details on:** 0151 225 2498.

First Sunday: Manchester to Blackpool Veteran and Vintage Car Run. Blackpool cavalcade early afternoon. **Details on:** 01565 621113.

Mid-June (usually Sunday): Manchester Lord Mayor's Parade. Big city centre procession sets off around noon. **Details on:** 0161 234 3763.

Second Saturday: King Cotton Carnival, Burnley town centre.

Mid-June (Saturday): Rudyard Lake Regatta, Rudyard, near Leek.

Third Sunday: Rossendale Carnival, Bacup. Procession between Bacup and Waterfoot.

Late June: Liverpool's Hope Street Festival of Art. **Details on:** 0151 281 0010.

Last Saturday: Southport Charity Carnival, town centre.

Last Saturday: Oldham Charity Carnival and Parade, Alexandra Park.

JULY
First Saturday: Altrincham Festival parade from town centre.
First weekend: Glossop Dale Carnival and Country Fair, Glossop, Derbyshire.

First week: River Carnival and Raft Race, River Dee, Chester. Details on 01244 317962.

Second weekend: Preston Maritime Festival, Preston Dock. Tall ships, displays and fireworks.

Second weekend (two days): Wirral Show, New Brighton. Free event.

Mid-July (Saturday): Congleton Carnival. Hour-long procession through town centre. Carnival held every two years in even years.

Late July: Fleetwood Transport Festival.

Last Sunday: Greater Manchester Police Open Day. Hough End Fields. Mauldeth Road West, Chorlton-cum-Hardy. Big show with two entertainment arenas, starting late morning. Fairground, free entry and car parking.

Last Saturday: Oldham Charity Carnival and Parade.

Last weekend: St Helens Show, Sherdley Park.

AUGUST

First Sunday: Blackpool Carnival Parade along promenade (starts around 10.30 am)

First weekend (Saturday, Sunday): Morecambe and Lancaster Bands Festival in streets.

Mid-August (Sunday): Macclesfield West Park Family Fun Day. Multi-arena entertainments and 250 stalls.

Last Saturday and Sunday: Southport Air Show over sea front. Car parking on the beach.

Late August (Saturday and Sunday): Haslingden Street Fair, Haslingden town centre, near Accrington.

Last Saturday: Crewe and Nantwich Carnival in Queens Park, Crewe.

Last Sunday: Family Fun Day in Queens Park, Crewe.
Details on: 01270 537239.

Last Days of August to 31 October: Matlock Bath Illuminations and Venetian Nights. Illuminated boats on river Derwent and fireworks.

Last week: Georgian Festival and National Sedan Chair Carrying Championships at Lancaster.

Bank Holiday Monday: Bolton's Victorian Street Fair. Around a hundred stalls manned by people in Victorian costume surround Bolton Town Hall. Entertainment in Town Hall square.

SEPTEMBER

First weekend: Glossop Victorian weekend. Craft stalls, street entertainment.

First Saturday: Eyam Carnival in Derbyshire.

First week: Blackpool Illuminations switch-on. Lasts until the first week in November.

First Sunday: Vintage transport rally in Heaton Park, Manchester. Vintage buses and other vehicles start from Museum of Transport in Boyle Street, Cheetham.
Details on: 0161 205 2122.

September-October: Manchester Festival. Annual live arts event, including many free events.

Second Sunday: Castlefield Carnival, Manchester. Free outdoor entertainments, stalls, narrow boats rally on canal basin at Castlefield, off Deansgate.
Details on: 0161 834 4026.

Mid-September: Heritage Open Days. The Civic Trust co-ordinates nationwide free admission opening of historic buildings not normally open to the public. Usually second weekend in September. Contact local Tourist Information Centres or Civic Trust for details of regional events.

Mid-September: National Trust free entry day for many properties.
Details on: 01743 709343 or Ambleside on 01539 435599 of this mid-week concession from regional offices in Shrewsbury.

Mid-September: Vintage Vehicle Cavalcade, Helmshore Textile Museum, near Rawtenstall.

Last Sunday: Rossendale Valley Motorbike Show. Around 1,000 veteran, vintage and modern machines are on display at Rawtenstall.

Last Sunday: Morecambe Heritage Gala.

Last Sunday: New Brighton Classic. Annual gathering of vintage, veteran and classic cars on promenade (All day).

OCTOBER

October 1-31: Visionfest, Liverpool's annual visual arts and design festival. Over 150 exhibitions and events.
Details on: 0151 708 9887.

NOVEMBER
First Saturday: Lancaster Fireworks Spectacular and Lighting of Beacon.

Early November: Bonfire and Fireworks Display, Queens Park, Crewe.

Mid-November: Manchester Christmas Lights switch-on in Albert Square.

Late November to early January: Castleton Christmas Lights at Castleton, Derbyshire.

The author will be interested to know from readers about any important changes concerning free admission places in the book, or about new free admission places which are not in the book, or which have opened since publication.

He would also be grateful to hear about closures of free admission places or about free admission places in the book which have imposed new admission charges.

Readers are invited to sent written information to Pen and Sword Books Ltd., 47 Church Street, Barnsley, for onward transmission to the author.

TOURIST INFORMATION CENTRES

Accrington	Town Hall, Blackburn Road.
	Telephone: 01254 872595
Altrincham	20 Stamford New Road.
	Telephone: 0161 912 5931
Ashton-under-Lyne	32 Market Street.
	Telephone: 0161 343 4343
Barrowford	Park Hill
	Telephone: 01282 666704
Birkenhead	Woodside Visitor Centre, Woodside Ferry Terminal.
	Telephone: 0151 647 6780
Blackburn	King George Hall, Northgate.
	Telephone: 01254 53277.
Blackpool	Visitor Centre, 1 Clifton Street.
	Telephone: 01253 478222
Bolton	Town Hall, Victoria Square.
	Telephone: 01204 334400
Burnley	Burnley Mechanics, Manchester Road.
	Telephone: 01282 664421
Bury	The Met. Arts Centre, Market Street.
	Telephone: 0161 2535111

Buxton	The Crescent. *Telephone:* 01298 25106
Chester	Town Hall, Northgate Street. *Telephone:* 01244 402111.
Chester	Visitor Centre, Vicars Lane. *Telephone:* 01244 402111.
Clitheroe	12-14 Market Place. *Telephone:* 01200 425566.
Congleton	Town Hall, High Street. *Telephone:* 01260 271095.
Fleetwood	Old Ferry Office, The Esplanade. *Telephone:* 01253 773953.
Garstang	Council Offices, High Street. *Telephone:* 01995 602125.
Glossop	The Gatehouse, Victoria Street. *Telephone:* 01457 855920
Knutsford	Council Offices, Toft Road. *Telephone:* 01565 632611
Lancaster	29 Castle Hill. *Telephone:* 01524 32878
Liverpool	Atlantic Pavilion, Albert Dock. *Telephone:* Special Premium Line on: 0906 6806886 (Info.)
Lytham St Annes	290 Clifton Drive South. *Telephone:* 01253 725610.
Macclesfield	Town Hall. *Telephone:* 01625 504114.
Manchester	Visitor Centre, Town Hall Extension, Lloyd St. *Telephone:* 0161 234 3157/8.
Morecambe	Old Station Building, Marine Road. *Telephone:* 01524 582808.
Nantwich	Church House, Church Walk. *Telephone:* 01270 610983.
Northwich	1 The Arcade. *Telephone:* 01606 353534.
Oldham	11 Albion Street. *Telephone:* 0161 627 1024.
Peak District	Peak National Park Information Centre, Bakewell. *Telephone:* 01629 816200.
Preston	The Guild Hall, Lancaster Road. *Telephone:* 01772 253731.

Rawtenstall   41-45 Kay Street.
                   Telephone: 01706 226590.
Rochdale   The Clock Tower, Town Hall.
                   Telephone: 01706 356592
Saddleworth   Saddleworth Museum, High Street, Uppermill.
                   Telephone: 01457 870336.
Salford   Salford Quays.
                   Telephone: 0161 848 8601.
Southport   112 Lord Street.
                   Telephone: 01704 533333
Stockport   Graylaw House, Chester Gate.
                   Telephone: 0161 474444.
Warrington   21 Rylands Street.
                   Telephone: 01925 442180
Wigan   Trencherfield Mill, Wallgate.
                   Telephone: 01942 825677.